PRO MOTOCROSS

AND OFF-ROAD
RIDING TECHNIQUES

DONNIE BALES
WITH
GARY SEMICS

MOTORBOOKS
INTERNATIONAL

Dedication

To the memory of Danny Hamel, Wayne Cornelius, Jeff Barbacovi, and Mark Gleckl—four enthusiasts and friends who lost their lives during 1995. You will be forever missed.

This edition first published in 2000 by Motorbooks International, an imprint of MBI Publishing Company, Galtier Plaza, Suite 200, 380 Jackson Street, St. Paul, MN 55101-3885 USA

© Donnie Bales, 2000, 2004

Motorbooks International titles are also available at discounts in bulk quantity for industrial or sales-promotional use. For details write to Special Sales Manager at Motorbooks International Wholesalers & Distributors, Galtier Plaza, Suite 200, 380 Jackson Street, St. Paul, MN 55101-3885 USA.

ISBN 0-7603-1802-6

Project Editors: Lee Klancher and Lindsay Hitch
Layout by Chris Fayers

Printed in China

On the front cover: Ricky Carmichael is hailed as the greatest motocross racer of all time.

On the frontis: Heavy-duty chain guides help keep power going to the rear wheel. It's also important to keep the chain tight and both axle adjusters even to avoid premature wear.

On the title page: Though it's not easy to gauge, strive for the shallowest point to make a water crossing. Wheelying across can be a good way to keep dry, but the resistance of the water will pull the front end down. Also, be certain that the bottom of the river is relatively smooth—a hidden log or rock could give you a quick trip over the bars and into the drink.

On the back cover: [Right] Proper riding technique affects everything from the starting line all the way to the checkered flag.
[Left] The only way to become a champion is through practice, and more practice. Just ask Ricky Carmichael, the winningest rider in AMA history.

WARNING: Off-road motorcycle riding is an extremely dangerous and sometimes fatal sport. The riders depicted in this book are professionals using proper protective gear under controlled conditions. Attempting to duplicate their actions may be hazardous. Readers are cautioned that individual abilities, motorcycles, racetracks, terrain, weather, and riding conditions differ, and due to these unlimited factors beyond the control of the authors, photographers, and riders quoted in this book, liability is expressly disclaimed. Do not attempt any maneuvers, stunts, or techniques that are beyond your capabilities.

About the author: Donnie Bales has been a freelance journalist for the last decade. He's a regular contributor to *Dirt Rider* magazine, and has been published in *MXracer*, *ATV Rider*, *Cycle News*, and *Team Green News*. He's produced three off-road motorcycle videos featuring Greg Albertyn, Steve Lamson, and Trevor Vines, and has served as an ESPN cameraman for the AMA 125/250cc National Championship MX Series. Bales has been riding off-road motorcycles for more than two decades, races motocross and off-road, and recently took up the hybrid sport of supermoto.

Gary Semics was a factory motocross racer for nine years and has been training riders for more than 20 years as owner and operator of the Gary Semics Motocross School. He's also known for his work as the personal trainer for several top riders, including Jeremy McGrath. Gary is originally from Lisbon, Ohio, where he grew up on his parents' farm. From 1972–1981, Gary was a factory rider for five different manufacturers (Can-Am, Honda, Husqvarna, Kawasaki, and Suzuki). He was always a strong contender, finishing consistently in the top ten. In 1982, Gary began racing the 500cc World Championship Grand Prix. His best year was 1982, with a respectable seventh in the 500cc series. The Gary Semics Motocross School was born in 1985.

Contents

by Ken Faught, Dirt Rider *editor-in-chief*

In 2003, I did an interview with *60 Minutes II* and tried to explain to them why I love motorcycles so much. It's hard for a 34-year-old adrenaline junkie to convince a 50-something hard-core CBS reporter why we play in the dirt every chance we get. I spent two hours talking to this veteran war reporter, and I think I finally got through. But along the way I was reminded why I started, and I was inspired to set more personal goals for my riding future and the fun I intend to find.

I explained my belief about going through different stages in life—how I was fixated with motocross racing during my teenage years and early 20s, before learning about the dynamic world of off-road. Racing was a mental break during the 10 years I spent in college, and it taught me a lot about things like budgeting, motivation, and decision-making. It taught me about success and failure, sacrifices, and communication. As the parent of a seven-year-old, it reminded me of the creative ways my parents used my sport as leverage to improve my grades and shape my behavior.

A few years ago, I entered another stage of life. I've been able to use the sport to see the world and broaden my horizons. My job as the editor of *Dirt Rider* and a reporter for *Speed Channel* and the *Outdoor Life Network* has taken me to Africa, Costa Rica, Peru, Mexico, Canada, Spain, England, France, Switzerland, Austria, Czech Republic, and Slovakia. Off-road motorcycle riding has taught me about culture, lifestyle, and the importance of family and friends. It's served as an escape from the everyday hell that otherwise consumes our lives and from the problems we see with society every night on the news.

I also explained to the reporter that the overall enjoyment doesn't depend on being fast—it has to do with finding your comfort zone and being safe. That's why I feel it's important to understand riding techniques and how a motorcycle functions. Combined with attitude and a sense for adventure, these two ingredients are necessary in the recipe for fun. I hope you'll use this information to make the most of your off-road experience and will enjoy it as much as I do.

Few people have logged as many off-road miles as Ken Faught *(center),* **shown here with Randy Hawkins** *(left)* **and Malcolm Smith. As editor-in-chief of** *Dirt Rider,* **he's experienced everything from riding in Africa, Costa Rica, and Peru to competing in trials, pro hillclimbing, motocross, and the International Six Days Enduro.** *Joe Bonnello*

Acknowledgments

Though my name is listed as author, this book would not have been published without the assistance of a lot of friends. First off, I need to thank Ken Faught from *Dirt Rider*, who hooked me up with Motorbooks International and has been supportive and helpful throughout this project. I couldn't have done it without you, buddy. I would also like to thank Joe Bonello, Scott Hoffman, Karel Kramer, and Bryan Nylander for their photographic assistance, and Lee Klancher from Motorbooks International for providing me with a lot of insight during the production of my first book. The first edition of this book took over a year to produce, and it's entirely too much for just one person to conquer. It's hard to believe this is the best-selling off-road motorcycle book and that we're already on our third edition.

A special thanks is extended to the professional riders who lent their time and expertise to the production of the book: Greg Albertyn, Fred Bramblett, Dick Burleson, Danny Carlson, Ricky Carmichael, Guy Cooper, Mike Craig, Ty Davis, John Dowd, Doug Dubach, Danny Hamel, Scot Harden, Steve Hatch, Randy Hawkins, Doug Henry, Mike Kiedrowski, Mike Lafferty, Steve Lamson, Ron Lechien, Jeremy McGrath, Scott Plessinger, Chad Reed, Larry Roeseler, Rick Sowma, James Stewart, Scott Summers, Shane Watts, Travis Whitlock, and Kevin Windham.

Jeremy McGrath has pioneered many of today's riding techniques while chasing six supercross titles. He is considered the master of our sport, and his supercross supremacy may never be equaled.

Introduction

Off-road motorcycle riding is an incredible sport that blends mechanical genius with athletic ability, finesse, and patience. It offers a multitude of challenges for riders of all skill levels, and it rewards us with the opportunity to interact with Mother Nature. Most important, it's perhaps the most entertaining way you can spend your time. Off-road riding is fun, and that's why most of us do it.

The intention of this book is to help you improve your riding by applying the techniques of the world's faster riders and those developed by motocross instructor Gary Semics, an ex-champion racer who has served as Jeremy McGrath's personal trainer.

Riders such as Greg Albertyn, Dick Burleson, Ricky Carmichael, Guy Cooper, Ty Davis, John Dowd, Doug Henry, Steve Lamson, Jeremy McGrath, James Stewart, and Larry Ward are just a few of the top professional riders represented in this book. Inside, you'll see these riders executing the techniques that brought them success, along with their personal tips on riding.

The book is geared to apply to all types of off-road riding. It explores the high-flying world of supercross and the fast-paced action of outdoor motocross, plus cross-country and enduro racing, where survival is of paramount importance.

Improving your riding technique begins with getting comfortable. It also requires that you and the bike work together as a unit. The opening chapters deal with simply making you as natural and comfortable as possible, from a guide on gear to tailoring the bike to your body and riding style. The gear guide includes some tips on dealing with conditions, which will keep you riding through all that our friend Mother Nature can throw at you.

Perhaps the most important part of the book is the chapter on body position, which is key to riding well and is the single most common problem in off-road riding. If you get out of position, you'll struggle to find ways to correct. If you stay out of position, you'll spend all your time fighting the bike and, inevitably, fall behind. If your body is in the right place, the rest of the techniques follow more easily. Good body position makes riding more natural and enjoyable.

The ensuing chapters take apart the basics of braking, accelerating, cornering, whoops, and jumping. These skills are a critical part of any ride, and you'll find the basics of each technique, the inside scoop from the pros, and some advanced techniques from motocross instructor Gary Semics.

You'll find a basic system you can apply to different conditions. You'll also see that your riding skills will improve if you learn to blend techniques. The brakes can be used to hold a line in a corner, for example, and the throttle is a key part of how far and how high you jump.

Once you learn this basic system, you can apply it to any kind of riding. This book—or even a three-volume set—can't cover every situation you may encounter. Applying the basic techniques to new obstacles and situations—and the fact that those obstacles are never exactly the same—is what makes off-road riding so challenging and enjoyable.

The off-road section of the book deals with conquering the most common obstacles found on the trail or the enduro circuit. Top professionals such as Dick Burleson, Guy Cooper, and Ty Davis give you the inside track on scaling vertical uphills, fording streams, navigating brutal ruts, banging your bars through the trees, and more.

Though this book should make you a smarter rider as you develop your skills, never forget that your ultimate goal is to have a good time. For a few elite riders, off-road racing is a career. When they go to the track, their paycheck depends on where they finish. For the rest of us mortals, the difference between finishing up front or in the back of the pack is a hunk of chromed plastic and bragging rights. Find your own victories and enjoy yourself. You'll probably come home happier, and you might find that the only way to get to that next level is to relax and have fun.

The Professional Riders in This Book

A number of top-ranked professional riders lent their time and expertise to the production of this book. Not only do these guys make up the heart of this book, they also are the soul of the sport. They're the definition of fast and have dedicated their lives to stretching that definition to new limits.

Here's a list of the riders who helped out with the book:

Greg Albertyn
Corona, California
1992 and 1993 125cc World Champion
1994 250cc World Champion
1999 250cc AMA 250cc National Champion

Born in South Africa, Greg Albertyn first claimed fame on the European Grand Prix circuit. He came to the United States in 1995, but it took him a while to adapt to the hybrid supercross-style courses. His breakthrough came in 1999, when he won the AMA 250cc National Championship in one of the sport's greatest battles.

Dick Burleson
Traverse City, Michigan
Eight-time National Enduro Champion
Eight-time ISDE Gold Medalist

King Richard Burleson epitomizes the off-road rider. If he's not lifting, pushing, or pulling a motorcycle around a seemingly impossible trail, he's probably not having a lot of fun. DB's a rugged sort who loves torture and craves excitement. The word "impossible" cannot be found in his vocabulary, and he's also a master innovator. He's the lead off-road test rider for Moose Racing and for *Dirt Rider*. Only the great Malcolm Smith and Larry Roeseler match him in popularity and cannot surpass his greatness.

Danny Carlson
Sun City, California
1995 Kawasaki Race of Champions, R-up
1996 NMA Grand National 125cc
    Stock Intermediate Champion
1996 NMA Grand National 250cc
    Modified Intermediate Champion

Danny Carlson was one of the hottest mini riders in the mid-1990s and was so talented that Honda hired the teenager to help develop the first-ever CR80R Expert. Carlson now competes on the four-stroke national circuit and occasionally races AMA 125cc Nationals and supercross.

Ricky Carmichael
Tarpon Springs, Florida
1997–1999 AMA 125cc National Motocross
    Champion
1998 AMA 125cc Eastern Region Supercross
    Champion
2000–2003 AMA 250cc National Motocross

Champion
2001–2003 AMA 250cc Supercross
Champion

Ricky Carmichael is the greatest motocross racer of all time. On May 18, 2003, he tied Jeremy McGrath's all-time record for AMA wins at 89. A short while later, the talented speedster from Florida broke the record, and he should have no problem hitting triple digits in his win column.

Guy Cooper

Stillwater, Oklahoma
1990 AMA 125cc National Champion
1994 and 1996 ISDE Gold Medalist

A natural showman, Guy won fans across the globe with aerial antics and a hard-charging style that made him a legend in motocross and supercross. He later took his high-flying techniques to enduro, hare scrambles, and cross-country racing.

Mike Craig

Lakeside, CA
1991–1993 Mickey Thompson
    Off-Road Grand Prix Ultracross Champion

Mike is one of the flashiest riders on the circuit and one of the most talented jumpers. As a former member of Kawasaki's Team Green, he won three consecutive titles during the televised Mickey Thompson Off-Road Grand Prix Series, which also featured truck and ATV racing. Mike later went on to win the 1994 Tampa Supercross.

Ty Davis

Hesperia, California
1987 and 1988 125cc CMC Golden
    State Series Champion
1987 250cc CMC Golden State
    Series Champion
1990 AMA 125cc Western
    Regional Champion
1991 Four-Stroke National Champion
1993–1995 Baja 1000 Winner
1995 AMA National Reliability Enduro
    Series Champion
1995 Cycle News Rider of the Year
1996 Vegas to Reno Champion
Seven-time ISDE Gold Medalist

In 1999, Dirt Rider ranked Ty Davis as the third greatest rider of all time. As a former motocrosser, he is best known for being the last rider to beat Jeremy McGrath in a supercross championship. As an off-road racer

and a former member of Kawasaki's Team Green, Ty has won nearly every off-road championship plus the legendary Baja 500 and 1000.

John Dowd

Chicopee, Massachusetts

John Dowd earned his coveted factory ride with Team Yamaha after winning two 250cc AMA Nationals in 1994 (Millville, Minnesota, and Binghamton, New York) as a privateer. He now races KTMs for his own private team.

Danny Hamel

Boulder, Nevada
1992–1995 Hare & Hound Champion
1994 ISDE Medalist
Multi-time Baja 500 and 1000 winner

Before his tragic death during the 1995 Baja 500, Danny was considered the greatest desert racer in the United States. When high speeds were involved, the young Hamel was seemingly unbeatable. He is greatly missed.

Scot Harden

El Cajon, California
1981 Baja 1000
Multi-time ISDE Medalist
Multi-time Best in the Desert Vet Champion

As the vice president of KTM Sportmotorcycle, Scot is one of the fastest senior off-road racers in the world. He has earned the number one plate several times in Best in the Desert competition and was a member of the 1983 U.S. ISDE Trophy Team.

Steve Hatch

Phoenix, Arizona
1991 International Six Days Enduro
    Junior World Team Champion
1991 AMA Athlete of the Year
1994 AMA National Reliability
    Enduro Champion
Multi-time ISDE Medalist

As a member of the powerful Suzuki factory squad, Steve has shown his talents throughout the world. He has won several titles and has been a part of Team USA's ISDE effort several years running.

Steve Lamson

Pollock Pines, California
1995 and 1996 AMA 125cc
    National Champion

Steve Lamson has one of the best work ethics in professional racing, and that determination has earned him two National Championships as a member of Team Honda. In 1999, he moved to the 250cc class full-time as Jeremy McGrath's teammate in the powerful Chaparral Yamaha camp. In 2003, after a stint with Husqvarna, he moved to Suzuki's team, wearing the No. 6.

Ron Lechien

El Cajon, California
1984 Unadilla 250cc USGP winner
1985 AMA 125cc National
    Motocross Champion
1989 Hollister 500cc USGP winner
1989 member of the winning Motocross
    des Nations team

Ron is probably the only rider in the world to be born with the same amount of natural talent as Jeremy McGrath. Lechien's smooth technique and near-flawless style has made him a cult figure with diehard race fans. At age 16, Ron became the youngest rider to win a supercross when he won at Orlando on June 11, 1993. He went on to win seven more, plus dozens of Nationals.

Jeremy McGrath

San Diego, California
Motocross/Supercross
1993–1996, 1998–2000 Supercross
    Champion
1995 AMA 250cc National Motocross
    Champion
1991–1992 AMA 125cc West Supercross
    Champion
1994 member of the winning Motocross
    des Nations team.

Hailed as the most natural rider to grace the sport of motocross, Jeremy has won an unprecedented four straight 250 Supercross titles (six if you include his 125cc titles) and all but one round of the series in the 1996 season while riding for Team Honda. He won back-to-back titles once again in 1998 and 1999. With flawless technique and a habit of getting the hole shot and running away from the pack, Jeremy has dominated the competition like no other rider in the history of the sport. In 1995, he proved those who doubted his outdoor ability wrong by wrapping up the 250cc outdoor motocross title. McGrath retired on January 3, 2003, as the winningest rider in supercross history. With 73 stadium 250cc wins, his record may never be beaten!

Rick Sowma
Long Beach, California

Rick has worked as a mechanic for several privateers and even wrenched for Ty Davis part-time in 1995. With over four decades of experience, Sowma has seen it all and is always a great source of knowledge.

Scott Summers
Petersburg, Kentucky
1989 and 1996 International Six Days
  Enduro Gold Medalist
1990, 1992–1994 AMA Grand National
  Cross-Country Champion
1990 AMA Sportsman of the Year
1990, 1991, 1993, and 1995 AMA National
  Hare & Hound Champion

As Team Honda's most recognizable off-road team, Scott and his mechanic, Fred Bramblett, are a dominant force in woods racing and have become legendary for putting Honda's XR600R four-stroke into the winner's circle on a regular basis.

Travis Whitlock
Elizabeth, Colorado
1990 and 1998 World Cup Hillclimb
  Champion
Four-time Canadian Hillclimb Champion
Nine-time North American Hillclimb
  Association National Champion
Eight-time Great American Hillclimb
  Champion

In the extreme sport of hillclimbing, Travis Whitlock is one of the most celebrated riders in the sport's 85-year history. In addition to his many titles, he was the only rider to beat supercross champion Jeremy McGrath during a 2003 hillclimb event in Billings, Montana.

Larry Roeseler
Hesperia, California
1973–1976 AMA District 37 Champion
1989 AMA Hare & Hound 250cc Champion
1991 AMA National Reliability Series
  Champion
1985 CMC Four-Stroke National Champion
13-time ISDE Medalist (10 gold, 2 silver,
  1 bronze)
10-time Baja 1000 winner

As a member of Team Husqvarna and Kawasaki's Team Green, Roeseler was the dominant off-road racer in the pre-Ty Davis era. In fact, during Roeseler's career, which spanned more than a decade, he and Davis won Baja several times as teammates.

Gary Semics on Riding Techniques

The Gary Semics motocross techniques listed in this book are the result of more than a decade of Gary's work with a variety of riders, ranging from raw novices to the smoothest and most precise riders the sport has ever seen.

Over the years, Gary developed these techniques from a decade of riding professionally for a number of factory teams and from another decade of teaching motocross in his school. He also refined the techniques as a result of working with his star pupil, Jeremy McGrath.

These techniques, which Gary calls the absolute techniques of motocross, are the basic riding skills needed to excel. They're tailored specifically to motocross but apply to all types of off-road motorcycle riding.

All riders use their own style, but that style comes from these absolute techniques. For example, you may find that you favor the outside line in corners and carry a lot of speed through the corner. This is good when

Semics is the owner and operator of the Gary Semics Motocross School. He trains riders around the country, from beginners to top professionals.

Semics *(right)* is the personal trainer of multi-time champion Jeremy McGrath. The two have worked together since McGrath was an amateur.

Semics and McGrath look over some lines on the Yamaha supercross test track in California.

you have a clear track but doesn't work as well when you're in a lot of traffic. On the other hand, you may tend to come in hard, brake-slide to turn, and come out hard on the gas. This is good for passing but requires that you scrub off a lot of speed and hook up well to gain it back.

Both types of riders use the absolute techniques, the difference being how often they choose to use a particular one. The rider carrying a lot of speed, for example, would tend to use a little rear brake to hold a line, while the rider who squares corners would use the front and rear brake to place the front precisely.

The two fundamentals of motocross are maintaining the center of balance and mastering the use of all five controls.

Maintaining the center of balance deals with body positions and movements. This means that your body is always in the right place at the right time. When you've mastered this, the motorcycle becomes an extension of your body. You'll flow naturally from corner to corner. This is not only the fastest way to ride, it's also the most enjoyable and requires less energy.

Mastering the use of all five controls deals with proper control of the clutch, throttle, front brake, rear brake, and shifter. When you have precise control of these elements, you have ultimate control of the motorcycle. The key is being able to use several controls at once and to cut the transition between braking and accelerating to a minimum.

A good neutral body position is your foundation, and from there you can branch into proper body position while traversing other obstacles. Factor in using the controls and you have a formula for success for everything from corners to whoops to jumps.

Yes, this book will give you the basic techniques involved in motocross racing, but remember this: the reason the top riders are so fast is that they can do these techniques better than the rest. These techniques are ingrained in their nervous systems as reflex reactions. Repetition is the mother of skill. The more perfect practice you do, the better you get.

About Gary Semics

Gary Semics was a factory motocross racer for 10 years and has been training riders for more than 20 years as owner and operator of the Gary Semics Motocross School. He's better known, however, for his work as the personal trainer for several top riders, including Jeremy McGrath.

Gary is originally from Lisbon, Ohio, where he grew up on his parents' farm. He began racing professionally at age 17. He raced what was then the Trans-Am (Trans-America) series, which took him from one end of the country to the other. From 1972–1981, Gary was a factory rider for five different manufacturers (Can-Am, Honda, Husqvarna, Kawasaki, and Suzuki). He was always a strong contender, finishing consistently in the top ten. He won the 1974 500cc Supercross Championship for Husqvarna, several Nationals, and placed second and third in the 500 series in 1976 and 1979.

In 1982, Gary began racing the 500cc World Championship Grand Prix. These races featured the best riders in the world, competing in just about every country imaginable. His best year was 1982, with a respectable seventh in the 500cc series. After three years of traveling the globe, Semics decided it was time to come home and start a new avenue.

The Gary Semics Motocross School was born in 1985. From there it was Gary's quest to train motocross riders around the country. To reach all these motocross enthusiasts, he produced the Gary Semics Motocross Techniques Video Series.

In 1987, Gary began working with 16-year-old Jeremy McGrath, one of the legends of the sport. Gary continues to aid some of the top riders in the world, including Steve Lamson, Ezra Lusk, Brian Swink, Kyle Lewis, and Mike Brown.

Chapter 1

RIDING GEAR
How to Choose the Necessities

Off-road motorcycle riding involves a series of calculated risks. Though some are bigger than others, all are potentially dangerous. Fortunately, aftermarket companies have vastly improved the quality of riding apparel and now offer a wide array of high-tech protection equipment. But don't be fooled. Even when covered from head to toe in body armor, you can still get hurt.

Safety gear is designed to protect you from minor injury only. No piece of protective gear on the planet can offer 100 percent foolproof protection in any and all situations. Because of the variety of protective gear on the market and because the technology changes so rapidly, it's advisable to do your own research and ask your own questions before making a purchase. Check with your local dealer and ask some of your riding buddies what they've learned about riding gear.

To help get you started, this book provides information on some of the key items you should look for.

Helmet

A helmet is perhaps the most important piece of safety equipment money can buy, for obvious reasons. Helmets are designed to absorb some of the energy created during a crash or contact with other objects.

Most manufacturers claim that a helmet should fit snugly, so that it doesn't bounce around on your head, but it shouldn't be so tight that it causes discomfort. If you have any questions on sizing or safety

Helmets come in all shapes and sizes, with dozens designed for off-road motorcycle use.

issues, consult the helmet manufacturers directly, since they all have their own recommendations and concerns.

Helmets have come a long way from the days when they were open-face, unvented, and monochromatic. Modern helmets are loaded with features, including adjustable visors, ventilation channels, brilliant graphics, goggle strap holders, and removable liners for easy washing. There are too many helmets on the

market to list every one, but some are popular among racers and hard-core enthusiasts.

One of the most popular is Shoei's VFX-R. Though its approximate $400 suggested retail price is on the high end of the scale, many riders find it one of the most comfortable helmets, because it's also one of the lightest. Like many helmets, the VFX-R also features a removable liner and a vented mouthpiece.

Bell makes several good helmets, including its premiere Moto 7 line, but many riders find that some Moto 7 models feel heavier than some of the competition, even though on certain models the weight is comparable. Helmet weight is important, especially in off-road riding, because additional stress on the neck muscles fatigues you more quickly.

Another inherent characteristic of Bell helmets is a smallish fit. Some riders find that the lining fits snugly around the ears and pushes on cheeks. If this is a problem, it'll be apparent when you try on helmets at your local dealer. Bell helmets are reasonably priced and offer a wide variety of stylish graphics and some of the hottest racer replicas on the market, including the ever-popular McGrath lid.

Another major player in the helmet market is Arai, which has made a name for itself by producing a line of helmets with removable mouthguards. Though most riders use the mouthguard full-time, woods riders commonly remove it (making it an open-

In addition to providing protection, most riding gear is also stylish. James "Bubba" Stewart is decked in Fox gear at the Anaheim Supercross.

face helmet), to increase airflow. In general, Arai helmets are comfortable and provide a good fit.

Several other companies, such as AXO, KBC, HJC, Fox and O'Neal, produce quality helmets.

This is one area where you shouldn't necessarily shop for the best bargain. Also, new helmet regulations are in the works to make helmets safer, which will affect the size and shape of helmets in the not-too-distant future.

A helmet is designed to be buckled below your chin. It doesn't have to be tight, but it should be secure enough not to accidentally fly off your head while you're riding or in case of a crash. It may seem silly, but it happens more than you might think.

Goggles

Eye protection is vital, because of the extreme nature of the sport. Flying rocks, sand, dirt, twigs, bushes, and branches can temporarily, and sometimes permanently, blind riders. Goggles also reduce, and in most cases eliminate, the effect of wind on your eyes.

How to Set Up Goggles, No Matter What the Weather Conditions

Mother Nature can be downright brutal. One minute you can be shredding in loam, while the next you can be paddling your way through axle-deep mud. Just as weather determines bike setup and preparation, it also determines eye protection. Restricted vision can slow you down, and no vision stops you dead in your tracks.

While many people believe that goggle prep is as simple as cleaning the lens, they frequently overlook the multitude of variables and options. Truth is that there are hundreds of combinations to consider when you enter the world of Turbofans, tear-offs, Roll-Offs, frame choice, lens selection, and so on. The best way to determine what works best for you is to experiment. Either borrow from friends what you don't have or go to your local dealership and buy a supply of goggle accessories you think might be beneficial and then try different combinations.

Frame Choice

Many types of goggle frames are available: children's, adults', and over-the-glasses

Goggle frames come in various shapes and sizes, from over-the-glasses types to children's goggles. The most important consideration is that they fit comfortably inside your helmet and provide adequate peripheral vision.

An assortment of lenses is available for goggles, ranging from colored for different lighting conditions to no-fog.

goggles. Regardless of what brand, style, or size you choose, make sure the goggles fit comfortably inside your helmet and provide you with adequate peripheral vision. They should also fit your face, because facial features affect comfort and the goggles' ability to keep debris from entering the sealed goggle chamber. Eye port sizes vary wildly among helmet manufacturers and must be taken into consideration when making sure the goggles fit inside your helmet.

Lens Selection

Goggle manufacturers sell a variety of lenses designed for all types of weather conditions, varying both in color to help with lighting conditions and in thickness to reduce fogging. These are the most common:

CLEAR: The most popular lens, and the only lens the goggle manufacturers suggest for all types of riding.

GRAY OR SMOKE: Recommended by Scott

Vision is what goggles are all about, and a large dollop of roost is all it takes to blind you. The solution is to (a) hole shot every race or (b) get some tear-offs or Roll-Offs. Tear-offs, which are peel-off film, clear the entire goggle but wipe your vision only five to ten times. Roll-offs (shown) give you 30 feet of film to work with but clear only a strip of vision.

U.S.A., Smith Sport Optics, and Oakley for bright sun.

ORANGE: Recommended by Smith Sport Optics for overcast/muddy, overcast/dusty, and rainy conditions.

YELLOW: Recommended by Smith Sport Optics for overcast/muddy, overcast/dusty, and rainy conditions. Smith also suggests that a yellow lens should be a serious option for riding at night.

GRADIENT: A clear lens with a narrow band of smoke or gray at the top. This lens works like a bifocal for riding in bright conditions. In the normal position the lens is clear, but when you tilt your head down, the lens appears either gray or smoke (depending on the lens).

MIRROR: Used mostly in dusty conditions encountered with bright skies.

DOUBLE-PANE: Two clear lenses bonded together that reduce fogging. Double-pane lenses come in a variety of colors.

FOG-RESISTANT: A single-pane lens with small holes drilled around the edges, to allow airflow. The holes are covered with a microfiber cloth, intended to keep debris out of the eye port.

Face Masks

Face masks gained a lot of popularity in the early 1980s, before full-face helmets were common. Originally, they attached to the goggle and extended to chin level, to protect a rider's face from flying objects. Though most goggle companies still sell full masks for riders who prefer open-face helmets, a smaller version, known as a half mask, is available, which covers a rider's upper lip. The half mask is preferred for full-face helmets, especially on rocky courses.

Tear-Offs and Film Systems

When moisture is present, clear vision isn't usually in ample supply. Take mud, for example: one good douse of roost and your goggles are wasted. Tear-offs and Roll-offs, however, were designed to combat this vision ailment. Though tear-offs and Roll-offs work differently, both operate on the same principle. They use an ultrathin piece of plastic film that you discard when your vision is obstructed. Tear-offs consist of one or more (up to 10, depending on the manufacturer) sheets of film secured on top of the lens. When you need to clear the goggle lens, you take your left hand off the handlebar, grab a tab attached to the tear-off, and pull the sheet away from the goggle.

PRO SETUP TIPS
GOGGLES

Jeremy McGrath—"Check to make sure that your goggle foam isn't ripped. If it is, small pieces of debris could get inside and mess up your vision."

Ricky Carmichael—"I always like to have a couple tear-offs, just in case. There's really no reason you would ever want to race without having tear-offs ready."

Mike Healey—"When it gets hot, I will sometimes wear a bandanna to absorb sweat. This will make sure that drops don't run down my forehead and find their way into my eyes."

Danny Carlson—"When it's really muddy, I will make a tear-off to go over a set of Roll-Offs. I SuperGlue the tabs from Scott three-pin tear-offs onto the Roll-Off canisters and then put one or two tear-offs on. Usually the first lap is where you get roosted the most, especially if you have a bad start. By adding the tear-offs, you can insure good vision for a while and still have thirty feet of Roll-Offs to use afterwards."

Steve Lamson—"When you take your goggles to the starting line of any race, you should always place them inside a plastic baggie, so they don't get dirty."

Rick Sowma—"When it's extremely dusty, I sometimes apply a small amount of baby oil to my goggle foam, so that dust won't penetrate. This is the same principle as oiling your air filter."

Dick Burleson—"For a long time I didn't use goggles a lot. Before I got my eyes fixed, I needed to wear prescription glasses. Now I only wear glasses (non-prescription) when I don't really need roost protection but I'm worried about fogging. Moose Racing makes a wide variety of plastic sunglasses that are available in clear, gray, or yellow. They provide a lot of venting yet protect your eyes from debris and wind blast."

| LENS | | | | | | SET UP | | | | | | | |
CLEAR	SMOKE	ORANGE	YELLOW	GRADIENT	MIRROR	TEAR-OFFS (no.)	ROLL-OFFS	TEAR-OFF/ROLL-OFF	NO-FOG	RAIN X	ANTI-STATIC	FOAM OIL	HALF-MASK
BRIGHT SUN R	R			R	R	6	O	O	R		O		O
BRIGHT SUN/DUSTY R	R					3	O	O	R			R	O
BRIGHT SUN/MUDDY R	R					6	R	R	R	O			O
OVERCAST R		O	O			6	O	O	R			O	O
OVERCAST/DUSTY R		O	O		R	3	O	O	R		O	R	O
OVERCAST/MUDDY R		O	O			4	R	O	R	O			O
NIGHT R		O	O			4	O	O	R				O
RAIN R		O	O				R	R	R	R			O
KEY		R=Recommended		O=Optional									

Smith's Roll-Offs work in a similar fashion but don't clear the entire field of vision. Instead, they use a 1 1/4-inch-wide strip of film that clears debris. The system stores roughly 30 feet of new film in a weather-resistant canister on the right side of the lens, known as the supply side. Opposite is a take-up spool, connected to a small, spring-loaded cord. When you pull the string, the system advances film across the front of the goggle. The advantage is that Roll-Offs are equivalent to roughly 25–30 tear-offs. The drawback is that they clear only a thin band across the lens.

If you use Roll-Offs, also use the Smith's Roll-Off visor. This adhesive-backed plastic strip lies directly beneath the upper rim of the goggle and prevents dust, dirt, and mud from getting trapped between the film and the lens surface.

The Prescription Alternative

A California-based company called Pro-Vue modifies goggles to accept prescription lenses for certain types of eye problems. Pro-Vue's system will work with most major brands of goggles and with tear-offs and Roll-Offs. Pro-Vue, 357 Sandy Point Court NE, Rochester, MN 55906, 800-548-8354.

Water and Dust Repellents and No-Fog Cloths

When your riding plans call for rain, an automotive product called Rain-X could turn out to be your best friend. Applied to the exterior of a goggle lens, it disperses rain, sleet,

and snow for hours on end. You can order Rain-X direct or find it in most places that sell automotive supplies. Rain-X, 7428 East Karen Drive, Scottsdale, AZ 85260, 800-542-6424.

Like water, dust is one of the most difficult elements to deal with, because it gets everywhere. The most effective way to cope with dust is to use Mr. Moto Quick Polish repellent. The solution is sprayed on, then buffed out using a lens cloth. Quick Polish should be applied to both sides of the goggle lens, in case dust penetrates the goggle foam.

Another lens treatment is a no-fog cloth, a chemically treated cloth designed to reduce the effects of fogging. It's used to coat the interior and exterior of the lens and can also double as a lens cleaner.

Gloves

Since your hands operate most of the controls, such as the throttle, clutch, and front brake, it's critical to choose a glove you feel absolutely comfortable wearing. In general a glove should fit snugly, but not so tightly that it feels restrictive, especially in the web area at the base of your fingers. Also, the glove shouldn't be too big, or the excess material will reduce your sensitivity and ability to operate the controls. Make sure the gloves seal properly around the cuff, to keep debris from entering, but not so tightly as to cause arm pump. Some gloves have hook-and-loop straps around the cuffs, which are excellent,

but anxious riders often fasten them too tightly.

If you purchase gloves designed for off-road motorcycle riding, try on several brands. Motorcycle gloves have additional padding in the palms and usually a second layer of material on top of the hand. Depending on the quantity of padding and the type of material, some glove styles will be more comfortable than others.

Most manufacturers produce a lighter-weight glove for mud use. These are made mostly of cotton and have small rubber beads in the palm area for additional traction.

Jersey

Many motocross and off-road riders wear their jerseys a little loose, to avoid restricting movement. Most jerseys are made from cotton, but some companies, such as MSR, have been experimenting with breathable waterproof materials.

Regardless of the material, some riders stretch out the wrist cuffs, because the elasticity can hinder circulation, which has been linked to arm pump. Some riders, such as Ron Lechien, cut off the elastic part of the cuffs.

If the cost of a new $30–75 jersey is a deterrent, your dealer may have older gear in stock at a reduced price. Some companies, such as Fox Racing, also offer a budget line of clothing that looks stylish and, in many cases, provides the same fit as their more expensive line.

Kidney Belt

A kidney belt provides much-needed lower-back support and helps keep internal organs in place. Kidney belts should be worn fairly snugly around the waist, on top of the jersey but underneath the pants.

When buying a kidney belt, don't assume they're all the same just because they look alike. Kidney belts come in all shapes and sizes and are made out of all sorts of materials; some are even reinforced with plastic. Try various kidney belts on at your dealer to see what feels comfortable, and when you're doing this, make sure you try them on with your chest protector, because sometimes the two will interfere with one another.

Chest Protector

A chest protector is designed to shield you from roost thrown up by other riders. Though chest protectors that come with shoulder pads may also help protect the shoulders, most manufacturers don't make any claims as to the effectiveness of shoulder protection.

Chest protectors come in a variety of sizes and offer a wide range of protection. When choosing a chest protector, you ideally want to find adequate protection that doesn't restrict mobility beyond your liking.

Acerbis makes a chest protector called the Zoom that has plastic guards near the kidney area on each side, for additional coverage. They also manufacture a unique chest protector for women called the Lady Proton.

In addition to normal chest protectors, which cover the front and back of a rider's upper torso, some companies manufacture chest protectors that protect the front exclusively. Also common are chest protectors with a modular design (such as those by Answer, AXO, and Malcolm Smith), which allow biceps guards and back panels to be removed.

Riding Pants

In the sport's beginning, riding pants were constructed purely of leather, because it was the most durable material available. Over time, however, leather became too expensive (not to mention too hot in the summer), which pushed clothing companies to seek a variety of alternatives, including synthetics. Since the late 1970s, most pants have been constructed of nylon with polyester linings, along with removable hip pads and knee cups for additional protection.

Though the features are usually similar among the dozen or so manufacturers, sizing and cut is another story. Try on any pants you intend to purchase. Be sure they have enough room in the thighs, knees, and groin. You don't want the pants too loose, but you don't want them too tight, either. One of the most important things to make sure of when buying pants is that they're double-stitched for durability.

Pricing varies from $100-200, depending on style, size, and brand. While most pants hover in the $170 range, Fox Racing, Thor, MSR, and a few others produce two lines of pants on opposite sides of the price spectrum. The less expensive pants typically have fewer sewn-on graphics and are more generic but offer virtually identical protection to the manufacturer's more expensive line.

Look over carefully any pair of pants you intend to buy. Though quality control is excellent, every once in a while you may find a pair that's been cut improperly or has irregular sewing.

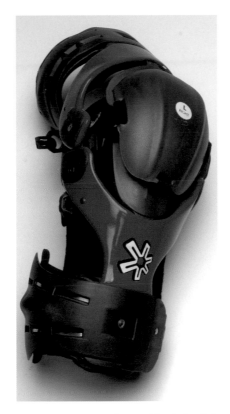

Knee braces such as this Asterisk are growing in popularity among riders. A pair sells for about $600 and is an excellent alternative to the custom-made CTi2 made by Innovation Sports.

Knee Braces or Knee Pads

For knee protection, you have two choices: either the knee and shin cups that come with most leathers or a knee brace. The knee braces on the market will fit most budgets and are becoming increasingly popular. Some knee braces may even be covered under your medical insurance if you've had a knee injury, so check on it before laying out any cash.

If you plan to use a knee brace instead of the traditional knee cups, they may not fit comfortably in all leathers. Because some apparel companies go for a tight fit around the knee, try on leathers with your knee braces before buying new pants. Riders who wear knee braces wear an amputee-style sock beneath them, to minimize chafing. A dozen or so companies offer knee braces designed for motocross and other high-risk sports. Off-the-shelf and custom-fit models are both available.

Boots

Off-road boots are incredibly durable and allow you to be confident that your feet and ankles can comfortably withstand a beating. However, their toughness makes them stiff and unyielding when compared to tennis shoes or other daily footwear. A good pair of boots is essential, because the foot and ankle take a lot of abuse. This is one item where it pays not to be cheap.

Some riders place insoles in their boots, to provide a little extra cushioning on hard landings. Insoles usually cost around $15 and slip into the boot.

Off-road riders will find that off-road jackets serve a variety of vital functions, primarily offering protection from the elements. Most are made out of water-resistant materials and do an excellent job of keeping you dry, but they also feature breather holes, so you don't overheat. *Lee Klancher*

One of the most popular models is Alpinestars' Tech 8, because of its excellent break-in and wear characteristics. The company's Tech 6 boot is also popular and is priced in the midrange of boots, with a street price in the neighborhood of $200. Alpinestars boots are so popular that companies such as MSR have their boots produced by the famed Italian company.

Sidi makes several types of boots, with something no one else offers: an option (for about $20 more) called the Sole Replacement System (SRS), which allows the soles to be changed once they get worn out from grinding on the footpegs.

You may also want to consider adding an insole that will make the boots more comfortable and lessen some of the impact of hard landings.

Socks

Many riders wear a pair of thick cotton tube socks that cover the entire calf. This reduces chafing that would normally result from wearing an ankle-high sock. Thick socks seem a bit odd in the heat of summer, but they're essential for keeping your feet dry and cushioned.

Some of today's high-tech fabrics can be helpful, especially for winter riding. Look for socks that are polypropylene lined, so they'll wick moisture away from your feet. This is especially important for long rides, when you'll be in the boots for half a day or more. You can also use thin polypropylene socks as a liner for heavier socks.

Enduro Jacket

Off-road jackets are a great way to keep the weather away in cool or rainy conditions. Most of these are Gore-Tex, which is ideal for off-road riding—when you're doused with rain or snow, it breathes and allows sweat to evaporate while keeping you dry.

Controlling body temperature is critical when riding. Less experienced riders tend to dress too warmly and forget that their body will warm up naturally while riding. Therefore, it's not uncommon to see riders with too many layers of clothing. This restricts their movements to the point where it may slow their reflexes.

Because temperature is critical, some companies produce enduro jackets with removable sleeves. This allows the jacket to be instantly converted into a vest.

Enduro jackets also offer plenty of storage space for maps, spare parts, snacks, and other items needed on the trail. The really high-tech jackets convert into a fanny pack for easy storage when it gets too warm to wear them, and they have openings for drink systems. Some even have a small built-in compass.

Fanny Packs

Fanny packs are a necessity for off-road riding, whether trail or racing. The tools and spare parts stored inside are often your only means of making repairs on the trail. The most important aspect is making sure you have enough parts, but not so much that the pack becomes too heavy to carry. If the items bounce around, fill up the space with a shop rag—which may come in handy on the trail.

Wear a fanny pack snugly around the

Fanny packs are a necessity for off-road riding, whether trail or racing. The tools and spare parts stored inside are often your only means of making repairs on the trail. Most motorcycle shops carry a variety of lightweight multi-use tools to save space.

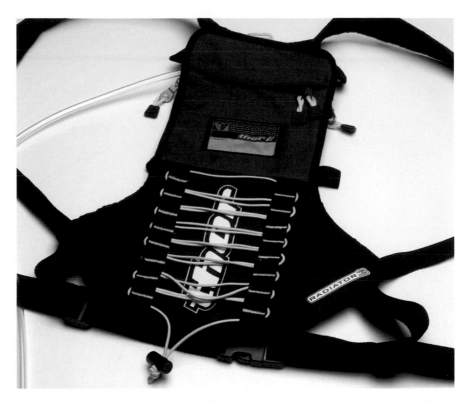

Even when the weather is cool, drink systems are important on long rides. Most are carried on the back and hold several quarts of fluid. Some riders carry bicycle-type squeeze bottles on the sides of their fanny packs.

waist. If it's too loose, it'll flop all over the place while you ride. Items typically carried in a fanny pack are Phillips and slot-head screwdrivers, pliers, wire cutters, spark plug(s) and spark plug wrench, wrenches (8, 10, and 12 millimeters) and sockets, knife, zip ties, electrical tape, safety wire, master link, driver's license, emergency cash, energy bars, and a small assortment of nuts and bolts. Many tools can be found in combination form to consolidate packing.

How to Dress for Temperature and Conditions

Inevitably, you'll come across weather that forces you to make a well-calculated decision on what to wear, be it cold, warm, or even stormy.

Typically, warm weather is the easiest to judge, because you can't strip down any further than the bare essentials. Some riders, however, wear a vented jersey or cut a hundred or so 1- to 2-inch slots on their jersey using household scissors.

Another way to stay cool is to carry water in either a backpack-style carrier or hip-mounted, bicycle-type squeeze bottle.

Selecting proper apparel for cold weather is much more difficult. The trick is putting on enough clothing to keep warm but not so much that you immediately become drenched in sweat. Dampness will make you cold and miserable for the rest of the ride.

The goal in staying warm is to stay dry. There are two keys to staying dry in cold

weather: layering and high-tech fabrics. If you dress in layers, you can peel off clothing as you warm up. If you're on the trail, a large buttpack or backpack can be helpful as a place to store clothing as you take it off.

Layering T-shirts and sweatshirts will get you by, but you'll still get wet with sweat and then get cold when you stop. Modern fabrics are the other, more important, part of the equation. Fabrics such as Gore-Tex make an ideal outer layer, because they prevent you from getting soaked with snow roost yet allow sweat to pass through them. The inner layer should be polypropylene or something similar, because these materials wick sweat away from your body, keeping you dry underneath. The combination turns cold-weather riding into a roost fest of long power slides that make you feel like Scotty Parker. With high-tech fabrics, you can get by with just poly underwear and a Gore-Tex jersey on 20-degree-and-above days.

By adding the following items to your regular riding gear, you can stay comfortable in a variety of cold temperatures. You'll cool off if you stop, so carry more clothing for a trail ride.

Polypropylene long underwear (top and bottom)
Long-sleeved turtleneck (optional)
Gore-Tex jersey
Gore-Tex riding pants (spray your regular riding pants with 3M Scotchgard or other water repellent as a cheap substitute)
Polypropylene sock liners
Heavy wool socks
Glove liners such as those made by UnderWARE
Enduro jacket (preferably Gore-Tex, with removable sleeves)

The Gore-Tex clothing isn't cheap, but it makes an enormous difference for winter riding and is durable enough to last you a lifetime. Gore-Tex clothing is also ideal for riding in rain. When there's a threat of moisture, many riders use an MSR Pak-Jak in mild temperatures or a Gore-Tex enduro jacket when it's a bit cooler. These are combined with either normal nylon riding pants or a Gore-Tex pant such as MSR's Pak-Pant.

You can find the poly long underwear, socks, and glove liners at a good outdoor store for a reasonable amount (Moose and UnderWARE also sell glove liners).

Chapter 2

MOTORCYCLE SETUP TIPS
The Most Critical Time You Can Spend with Your Bike

Over the last decade, motorcycle setup has become increasingly important as technology continues at an astounding rate. In addition to scheduled maintenance, a motorcycle must be set up properly for each rider. Everything from rider height, weight, style, and ability factors into the ever-developing formula of motorcycle setup. This information—combined with other variables, such as track and weather conditions and type of motorcycle—results in setup combinations and variables impossible to count.

Begin by fitting the motorcycle to the rider. When you're riding well, an off-road bike becomes an extension of your body. The two function as a unit, flowing with the terrain rather than fighting it. For this to happen, the motorcycle needs to fit you like a glove.

Motorcycle setup isn't a one-time job. Since so many variables are involved, setup changes on a daily and sometimes hourly basis, even if you're riding at the same place and in the same conditions. For this reason, it's a good idea to maintain a motorcycle setup log, to keep track of what works and what doesn't. Following is a description of the most common starting points for developing your personal preferences.

Handlebar

The handlebar may be one of the most important setup items, because it dictates how you'll be able to move around on the motorcycle. The aftermarket offers bars with a wide variety of heights and sweep.

Proper motorcycle setup is an absolute must because it determines how well your motorcycle works and, ultimately, how much fun you can have. This photo of Steve Hatch inside his home race shop in Scottsdale, Arizona, illustrates proper clutch- and brake-lever positioning. When his arms are in the attack position, the levers are almost at the same angle—just a little lower. This is a good starting point to determine your personal preference.

In general, taller riders prefer a taller handlebar, while those vertically challenged appreciate a lower bar. Riders have different tastes, so try different bars.

To get an idea of what suits you, loosen the bar clamps and rotate the bar on your bike out of the way. Then sit on the seat with the bike on the stand and get into your standard body position. Close your eyes and imagine reaching out and grabbing the handlebar. The imaginary

Jeremy McGrath is one of the best riders at setting up his machinery—one of the many reasons his riding style looks so effortless.

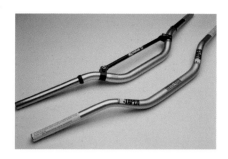

The latest trend in ultra-strong handlebars is an oversized lower tube. Renthal's Twinwall (above) and Answer's ProTaper (below) are arguably the strongest bars ever developed. Unfortunately, they also require the use of an oversized upper bar clamp and sometimes an entirely new upper triple clamp.

bar is close to ideal for you. Now you have to match a real bar to the one you visualized.

Rotate the bar back up and snug the bolts finger tight. Get into your standard body position again, close your eyes, and reach for the bars. You may find that the point you visualized earlier and the actual location of the bars are different. Adjust the bars, getting as close as possible to the bar you visualized. If the bar you're using can't be adjusted to that point, try a different bar. Ideally, take your old bar to the shop and compare it to new models. By comparing the two, you should be able to find a bar that suits your needs (a bit higher/lower, a little more sweep back, and so on.)

Your standard body position affects which bar you prefer. As your riding skills improve, so will your body position, so periodically check how your bars fit and make the proper adjustments.

Regardless of which bend you like, an aluminum handlebar is preferable, because of the strength. Steel bars are cheaper, but you can bend them easily. Aluminum bars, especially the better-quality units, are strong and justify the extra expense after a few simple get-offs. Among conventional handlebars, Renthal makes one of the most popular lines, race tested by many World and National Champions.

ProTaper bars from Answer Products have no crossbar and (as the name suggests) are tapered and much wider where the handlebar connects to the upper triple clamp. ProTapers cost about $80 a set, which doesn't include the hardware required to accept the thicker handlebar. If your bike has removable bar clamps, you may get away with spending about $50 for the extra parts, but if your machine has a solid clamp, it could cost you as much as $150. However, it will pay for itself in the long run if you're the type who normally bends handlebars easily.

Width is another way to tailor your bars to your needs. While motocrossers and desert racers usually prefer stock width (usually around 30–31 inches), cross-country and enduro riders tend to shorten the bars to 28–29 inches. This gives the bike a narrower profile, so it can fit between trees more easily. Note that the narrower the handlebar, the less control you have over the bike, because of the decreased leverage.

Once you've decided on the type of handlebar and the width, center the bars on the motorcycle and sit on the bike, to determine the angle of the handlebar before tightening the clamp bolts. Most riders prefer the bar ends parallel to the ground.

However, some riders, such as motocrosser Ricky Carmichael, run their bars incredibly low. It may look awkward, but it works well with RC's short stature and aggressive riding style.

Triple Clamp

Beginning in the 1990s, the aftermarket has offered triple clamps that change the location of the handlebar mount. This allows you to relocate the handlebar either closer or farther away. In some cases, it can also raise handlebar height. Some motorcycles already come stock with rubber-mounted bar clamps that can be rotated 180 degrees, to change the distance of the handlebar to the rider. Most changes are minor, but this is a way to fine-tune handling.

Triple clamp height can be so important that motocross teams test custom sets of upper clamps made in 1-millimeter increments to find the perfect setup for team riders. Though dozens of companies build triple clamps, the most common brands are Pro Circuit, Factory Connection, RG3, BRP, and Applied Racing.

This upper triple clamp has removable bar clamps that accept oversize bars, such as Twinwalls and ProTapers. The clamps are reversible, to change the relationship of the distance between bars and rider. Some companies even sell clamps that are shorter and taller, to give riders a wider range of customization.

Safety wire is a key ingredient for serious racers, used to double-lock grips and key fasteners.

Grips come in a variety of shapes, sizes, and rubber types. Since they cost only $10–15 and are the link to the most important set of controls, experiment to find what works best for you.

Handlebar Grips

Dozens of types of handlebar grips are available, and preferences vary wildly. To prevent blisters, some riders choose to shave several rows of ribs off the top of the grip. (This is not advisable when riding in wet conditions, because it reduces traction.) Motocrossers usually run a softer compound, while off-road riders tend to use harder compounds because of their excellent wear characteristics.

Grips should be glued to the handlebar using a grip glue and then safety-wired to the handlebar, to reduce the chances of a grip spinning and coming loose.

Levers

The clutch and front brake levers need to be easily accessible, both sitting and standing. If the levers are too high, they'll be difficult to use when standing. If they're too low, they'll be difficult to use when sitting.

As a starting point, sit on your bike with both perches loose enough to spin with minimal pressure. Position the levers at the same angle as your arms when sitting in the attack position and tighten to the manufacturer's recommended specifications. When in your standard riding position, your fingers should rest naturally on the levers. When your elbows are positioned correctly (slightly high), the levers will be pivoted forward. Be sure to assume a good body position when setting the levers.

Position the levers so their ends are about 3/8 inch from the end of the handlebar. This decreases the likelihood of a lever snapping during a crash. ASV and ARC sell innovative levers that fold forward in the event of a crash. These cost about $60 each, but they've proven incredibly durable in the racing world.

A Honda clutch lever and perch from a newer CR125 or CR250R work well for any brand. The Honda perches offer the closest thing to a perfect leverage ratio and can be adapted to fit most motocross and off-road bikes.

Clutch Perches

Aftermarket clutch perches accomplish a number of cool functions. The trickiest use a nylon bushing where the perch meets the bar. This allows the perch to be tightened, yet the entire assembly will spin on the bar in case of a crash. The perches also offer a quick-adjust feature, so cable tension can be adjusted mid-race, and many perches allow the reach of the lever to be adjusted inward or outward for different hand sizes. Four-stroke owners should note the availability of perches that incorporate hot-start levers into one assembly. This frees up space on the handlebar and makes things less crowded and more organized.

Seat

The seat is another part of the motorcycle that can be tailored to the rider, either with different seat covers or by modifying the foam. Though many riders stick with the stock seat, the aftermarket does make different foam densities. Seat covers are also available with a built-in gripping system that helps eliminate any unwanted sliding around. This seat is especially useful when gripping the seat with your knees, a critical aspect of riding, particularly in motocross.

If you're taller than average or suffer from knee problems, consider building yourself a taller seat using scraps of seat foam. Conversely, some shorter riders cut down their seats by carefully using a coarse kitchen knife. In fact, many supercross riders shorten the front of their seat so they can get better body positioning in the corners. If you shave off too much, though, you'll find that your butt gets pounded against the plastic seat base, which can be quite painful.

The clutch and brake levers should be positioned approximately 3/8 inch from the end of the handlebar to reduce the chances of the levers breaking during a crash. The best way to measure is to pull the lever as close to the grip as possible.

As a starting point, many riders position the shift lever so the bottom is parallel with the footpeg.

Many riders prefer to adjust the rear brake pedal height so it's a little lower than the footpeg.

Shift Lever

Adjusting the location of the shift lever is another way to tailor the bike to you. The lever can be moved in small increments, thanks to multiple splines on the shift shaft. Aftermarket shifters sometimes have different bends than the stock levers and are more economical than factory pieces. The aftermarket models are typically steel, which is slightly heavier but much more durable than the stock aluminum shifters.

Adjust the shifter so the bottom of the lever is on the same horizontal plane as the top of the footpeg. You may find that you prefer it a bit higher or lower, but you have to be able to shift from a sitting or standing position.

Brake Pedal

The location of the brake pedal is as important as that of the shift lever. As a starting point, adjust the brake pedal (in the resting position) so that the top of the pedal lies in the same horizontal plane as the footpeg. From there, tailor it subtly so you can use the pedal when sitting or standing. Once

adjustment is complete, make sure the rear brake doesn't drag. Brakes can drag when they're hot, so get the brakes good and warm (take a few laps using the rear brake hard), then double-check that they aren't dragging.

Tires

If you've ever watched a NASCAR race, you're probably keenly aware of the important role tires play in motorsports. Though many factory-backed riders use tires with special compounds, tire manufacturers have done an excellent job of producing off-the-shelf tires for a variety of conditions. Usually the best way to determine which one works best in your terrain is to see what other serious riders are using. The choice is always a matter of opinion, and even the tire manufacturers aren't always sure which will work best on a particular type of terrain.

No matter what the conditions, a worn-out tire gives bad results. Once the sharp edge of the knob rounds off, it loses grip. Top pros use a fresh set of tires for every moto; you'll have to make your own decision on how often to change tires. You can lengthen tire life a bit by flipping it on the rim, but braking effect will be lessened. Front tires typically last much longer than the rears, and different conditions are harder on tires than others. Just keep in mind that when the knobs get rounded off, you're losing traction.

Most tires are designed to run air pressure between 12 and 15 psi. The lower the air pressure, the better the traction, but also the more vulnerable the inner tube is to flats.

One way to reduce flats altogether is to install a solid foam insert known as a bib mousse. Michelin and Moose Racing both make these special puncture-proof bib mousses that cost between $100 and $130, and Dunlop is also producing a foam insert with a miniature inner tube inside.

Unfortunately, bib mousses are extremely difficult to install (requiring special tools and lubricants) and wear out fairly rapidly. While the manufacturers are working on ways to increase the life, the compounds break down with abuse and excess heat.

Bib mousses feel different from inner tubes, because they have different shock-absorbing characteristics. That is precisely why Dunlop has created the mousse that uses the small inflatable inner tube, so the sensitivity can be controlled.

BIKE SETUP

Jeremy McGrath—"I spend a lot of time testing different (external) gear ratios. It's amazing what kind of difference one tooth on the rear sprocket makes. Without proper gearing, your bike will never reach its fullest potential, because you'll constantly find yourself compensating with your riding style. When a bike isn't properly geared, you'll usually notice that you're constantly between gears and using too much clutch."

Steve Lamson—"It's really important to make sure that your brakes are working properly. I find it necessary to bleed the brake lines frequently, to avoid a mushy feel."

Mike Lafferty—"I like to make sure all my controls feel new all the time, so I lube my clutch cable on a regular basis, and when that is not enough, I install a new one."

John Dowd—"Replace your clutch perch and lever when it develops slop up and down. This is one good way to keep your bike feeling fresh."

Mike Healey—"When I'm setting up a new bike, I always experiment with different handlebar bends. I want something that complements the ergonomics of the motorcycle. In general, I usually pick what feels most natural."

Ty Davis—"For off-road, I use a braided front brake line. It's extremely powerful, because it has less flex than the conventional plastic lines."

Mike Healey—"I install beefed-up footpegs on all of my bikes. I like the wider feel of the Pro Circuit pegs over stock, plus I don't want to worry about a bent footpeg ruining my day."

Ty Davis—"When riding tight, slippery trails, I use a heavier flywheel. The added weight alters the power characteristics, by not allowing the engine to rev as fast as normal. This produces less wheel-spin and enables me to stay hooked up."

Mike Kiedrowski—"For more stopping power, I usually run an oversize front brake rotor on my race bikes."

Dick Burleson—"I think it's important to really know how your bike works. Study anything and everything. This way, you can feel when something is going wrong. It will also help you when you have to make creative trailside repairs. I really feel that guys who don't know much about mechanics are at a huge disadvantage in this sport."

Ken Faught—"Just because your bike feels good one day, don't think it'll last forever. Bike setup can change from day to day or track to track. When I ride off-road, I always try to think about how my bike is handling and whether there are any ways to make improvements. Sometimes a big improvement can mean adding two millimeters to the shock sag or lowering the fork in the triple clamp. I'm a firm believer that experimenting is the key to achieving good bike setup."

Jeremy McGrath—"I'm amazed at how many riders don't realize they can make their bike work better by fine-tuning the suspension. Stock bikes are good, but they are built for a wide range of riders. That's why there are dozens of rebound and compression settings on the fork and shock—to customize performance."

Tire choice is critical and must be taken seriously. Bridgestone, Dunlop, Metzeler, Michelin, and Pirelli make some of the best products on the market. While it's key to use a compound and tread pattern that match conditions, it's more important to have fresh rubber on your bike. When the knobs round off, you're getting less than optimum traction.

You can change the way your bike steers by raising or lowering the fork tubes in the triple clamp. When they're up like this, the bike corners more tightly, but you lose a little high-speed stability. When the fork is lower in the clamp, you gain stability but lose agility. This triple clamp has adjustable handlebar risers, to change the height and position of the bar.

Suspension

Suspension setup is the most critical element of motorcycle setup. Spring rate, oil levels, internal valving, rebound and compression damping settings, preload, sag, and especially motorcycle type can make all the difference in the world as to how a bike handles. Due to the extreme complexity involved, refer to your owner's manual or to the book Motocross and Off-Road Motorcycle Performance Handbook (see appendix for details) for guidelines. An entire book can be written on suspension setup alone.

Serious recreational riders and racers usually have their suspensions set up by an aftermarket company before fine-tuning in the field. If you decide to have your suspension modified, check with other riders to see what aftermarket companies are doing the best work for your type of bike. Hundreds of suspension companies are scattered throughout the United States, and each has its own opinion of what works and what doesn't.

Fork Tube Height

Many riders raise their forks 5–10 millimeters in the triple clamp. For quicker turning, the tubes can be raised even further (until they hit the base of the handlebar). The drawback is that this decreases high-speed stability and may cause headshake. Conversely, lowering the fork tubes (to where the upper tube is flush with the top of the upper triple clamp) gives you greater high-speed stability at the sacrifice of turning ability.

Guards

Several types of guards are available to protect your motorcycle from impact damage. Typically, motocrossers don't require as much armor as off-road riders, but most of these pieces are useful for any kind of riding. Works Connection is the most popular manufacturer in this arena. The company's fit and finish is exceptional, and they're the preferred source for many factory teams.

Skid Plate

The most common type of skid plate is a glide plate, a flat aluminum plate that protects the bottom of the engine and most of the frame rails. Larger versions, which wrap around the frame rails and protect the water pump cover or even the exhaust pipe, are also available. Off-road riders typically use the larger skid plates, while motocross racers favor the trim, light glide plates.

Pipe Guard

The pipe guard, used primarily by off-road riders, is a plastic or metal guard that wraps around the front lower section of the exhaust pipe, to keep it from getting dented.

MOTORCYCLE SETUP CHART

GENERAL DATA

Date:_____ Location:_____ Air temperature:_____ Humidity:_____Elevation:_____

Description of terrain and conditions:_____

SUSPENSION

Fork spring rate:_____ Fork oil level:_____ Fork compression (number of turns out):_____

Fork rebound damping (number of turns out):_____

Fork tube height (distance from top of fork tube to triple clamp):_____

Shock spring rate:_____

Shock low-speed compression (number of turns out):_____

Shock high-speed compression (number of turns out):_____

Shock rebound damping (number of turns out):_____

Shock sag:_____ Shock preload:_____

CHASSIS

Handlebar type: _____ Handlebar bend: _____

Handlebar width:_____ Grip type: _____

Front tire: _____ Front tire pressure: _____

Inner tube or bib mousse: _____

Rear tire: _____ Rear tire pressure: _____

Seat cover type: _____

Front brake pad brand and type: _____ Rear brake pad brand and type: _____

ENGINE

Fuel type:_____ Premix oil brand and ratio (if applicable):_____

Main jet:_____ Needle jet:_____ Pilot jet:_____

Clip position (from top):_____ Air screw (turns out):_____

Air filter brand:_____ Air filter oil brand:_____

Gear oil type:_____

MISCELLANEOUS

List of special accessories (i.e., handguards, skid plate, etc.):

Comments on how the bike worked (things you liked and disliked):

Heavy-duty chain guides help keep power going to the rear wheel. It's also important to keep the chain tight and both axle adjusters even, to avoid premature wear.

A wide assortment of guards is available to protect motorcycles against abuse. This skid plate by Works Connection is designed for motocross. It easily bolts on in less than 10 minutes and protects the bottom of the frame and engine. Larger engine guards, designed for off-road use, protect the engine cases, lower frame rails, and water pump cover.

If you plan to ride on public lands, make sure your bike is equipped with a spark arrestor, which is the law. Spark arrestors are stamped with a U.S. Forestry approval somewhere on the canister. This exhaust is a closed-course-only model used for racing and does not have a spark arrestor inside.

Gearing is one of the easiest ways to customize power. Adding a tooth to the rear sprocket will increase acceleration but will reduce top speed. In contrast, subtracting one tooth will increase top speed but will mellow throttle response.

Radiator guards are commonly used for both motocross and off-road. In addition to protecting the radiator from flying debris, the framework of the guards makes the entire radiator stronger and less susceptible to bending. A new radiator sells for about $250. A pair of guards goes for about $70. You do the math.

Frame Guard

Motocross and off-road riders use frame guards to protect the lower portion of the frame, near the swing-arm pivot bolt. The right side unit also protects the rear brake master cylinder from minor damage. Frame guards will keep paint from wearing off your frame and, in combination with a skid plate, can lengthen your frame's life.

Front Master-Cylinder Guard

The front master-cylinder guard is a small aluminum guard used by motocross and off-road riders to protect the front master cylinder. Compare the cost of these guards to that of a new master cylinder and you'll see why they're useful.

Radiator Guards

Although radiator guards have long been used by off-road riders, they're gaining popularity among motocrossers. The dual aluminum vented plates keep rocks, branches, and other objects from damaging ultra-expensive radiators. A pair of radiators can cost $600 to replace, and the aluminum guards are one-tenth that price.

Bark Busters

Bark busters are metal guards that protect the hands of woods riders from impact damage by trees. They also make the handlebar sturdier.

Hand Guards

Hand guards are plastic shields that protect hands from flying debris, such as rocks and mud. They're most often used by off-road riders and anyone riding in cold or muddy conditions. In cold weather, they also keep your hands warm. Some companies sell an optional spoiler kit that shields your hands a bit better.

Disc Guard

Usually made of plastic but sometimes of aluminum, a disc guard is designed to keep the rotors of motocross and off-road bikes from getting pitted or dinged. Some manufacturers even include disc guards on production machinery.

Shark Fin

Primarily used by off-road riders, a shark fin is a solid piece of metal, usually aluminum, that protects the rear brake rotor from impact damage.

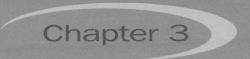
Chapter 3

TERRAIN AND CONDITIONS
A Sampling of What Mother Nature Has to Offer

Throughout your journeys, you're likely to encounter a variety of terrain: sand, shale, rock, mud, grass, water, hard-pack, loam, water crossings, tree roots, and so on—at various angles and speeds and during all sorts of weather conditions. When you combine temperature, moisture, snow, wind, humidity, and whatever else Mother Nature throws at you, you can encounter a vast number of obstacles.

As a rule, never go faster than feels comfortable, especially in unfamiliar terrain. While motocross and supercross have their own brutally tough man-made obstacles, Mother Nature is full of natural booby traps that will punish you for riding beyond your limits. Therefore, it's critical to have plenty of room to stop, in case you approach something that could cause you harm.

Whenever you ride in a new area, be extremely careful. Cruise around the area at a moderate pace until you feel comfortable reading the terrain. Here's an idea of what you may encounter:

Baked Mud

When certain types of mud dry out in the sun, they acquire a cracked crust. Although baked mud usually breaks apart easily and yields mediocre traction, it can sometimes be quite slippery, especially under braking or while turning. It all depends on the thickness of the dried layer of topsoil. If it's really thick, the top layer may slide around on top of the solid soil beneath. Treat it with caution.

Baked mud makes for interesting designs, but it can be dangerous. While it usually breaks apart with moderate pressure, sometimes it will withstand the weight of a bike, become unstable, and shift around.

Barbed Wire

Anywhere barbed wire is present is a threat to man and machine. Barbed wire can cause flat tires, get entangled in your bike, or rip you off the seat. Though it can be extremely difficult to see, use common sense and pay attention to any signs that may clue you in. Look for scraps left on the ground, and pay attention when riding near farms or other property that's sectioned off. A row of fence posts is also a clue that barbed wire is not far away.

Always keep an eye out for barbed wire. It's nearly invisible, even at low speeds, and is a favorite of farmers, ranchers, and home-owners for marking boundaries.

The variations in terrain are what make riding such an incredible experience. One of the most enjoyable aspects is searching for new obstacles to conquer. *Bryan Nylander*

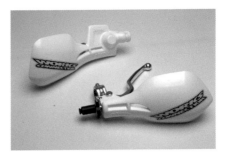

Motocross-style hand guards are lighter weight than those typically used in off-road. These, built by Works Connection, are designed to be used with an adjust-on-the-fly aftermarket clutch perch.

Wraparound hand guards such as these protect your levers and controls from impact damage and also keep your hands clean longer in a mud ride. Left: Vines are notorious for ripping riders off their bikes. Most of the time vines are difficult to see, because they're most common in shaded areas.

Bushes

Though most bushes are harmless, be careful. Bushes are a great hiding place for football-size rocks and holes. Some are strong enough to rip you off your bike if you try to punch through them.

Cacti

When your arm looks like it's been run through a cheese grater, you'll know you hit a cactus. Unlike what you see in movies, a cactus doesn't always look menacing.Many look absolutely harmless while in bloom. If you plan to ride in a desert-type area, find out what the cacti look like before you get stung.

Downhills

Even when you're prepared, downhills can be tough to tackle. Braking is tricky, and the pucker factor of dropping off a 70-foot cliff tends to break your concentration. This effect can be amplified when downhills become an accidental excursion. If you're riding around elevation changes, be alert!

Drop-Offs

This obstacle usually catches people off guard, because they're not paying close enough attention to the terrain. If you can't

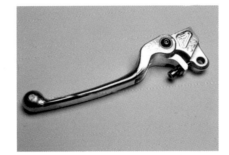

This is a forward-folding front clutch lever by ARC, one of the latest innovations in off-road. It's designed to fold forward instead of bending or breaking in case of a crash. Riders can also adjust the "reach" of the lever by adjusting the large screw. This cool but unnecessary feature allows the lever to be adjusted inward or outward for different hand sizes.

see the ground in the distance, don't assume it's all there. Slow down to a safe speed and approach with caution.

Dust

If it's dusty, don't ride blind. Slow down or come to a complete stop somewhere off the racing line. Sitting still in the midst of

This clutch perch, shown upside down for illustration, includes an adjuster that allows cable slack to be removed while riding and a hot-start lever for four-stroke riders. It also has a nylon bushing instead of the tight, clamp-like grip normally associated with metal-on-metal contact. This allows the perch to slip on the bar in case of a crash.

Radiator braces sell for about $70 and make the structural integrity of radiators much stronger. They're easy to install and are cheap insurance.

dusty track is a good way to get T-boned. If you're racing, consider straying off the main line (if it's safe), because many times the dust coming from another rider's bike will be isolated in a narrow band.

Fog

Treat fog like dust. Slow to a speed you feel is safe, or come to a complete stop if necessary. Fog can reduce visibility to zero, making it one of the most dangerous riding conditions.

Grass

When dry, grass provides loads of traction. However, when it's wet, it can be extremely slippery. When you're on wet grass, treat it like ice. Stay loose, initiate turns gradually, and be ready for either wheel to slide. Early riders beware: morning dew wets the grass considerably.

Gravel

Riding over gravel is like riding over marbles. Though it may seem harmless, don't underestimate its capability to rip you off your bike and pummel you into the ground. Again, stay loose and initiate turns more carefully. Also note that roosting in gravel is a good way to tear the corners of your fresh rear knobby.

Hardpack

This surface usually offers little traction, which makes acceleration, braking, and turning slightly more difficult than normal. Though it doesn't require watching out for anything special, remember you can always get hurt, no matter what you're doing or how safe conditions appear. Here's a place where tires can make a huge difference. Hardpack tires have larger cornering knobs and a compound that will allow you to ride with more confidence and traction.

Ice

Pay close attention when ice is present. If you come in contact with it, you'll most likely end up on the ground. Like the type of ice that forms in a puddle of standing water, frozen soil also has almost zero traction. In cooler temperatures, the ground freezes and becomes a near tractionless and rock-hard surface. Trelleborg ice tires or studding your own tires can give you surprisingly good traction on ice, although they'll still slide around a bit on frozen ground.

Mud is by far the messiest type of terrain you'll encounter and therefore requires special attention. In addition to the goggle-prep tips you learned about in Chapter One, riding in mud requires special preparation so your bike can survive. *Massimo Melani*

Perhaps the most important setup tip for riding in mud is to make sure the air box is sealed. If water gets into your engine, it'll create all sorts of problems.

Many top riders use porous foam to fill all crevices where mud can accumulate. The idea is to keep mud from adhering to your bike, so it doesn't add weight. According to Scott Summers' mechanic, Fred Bramblett, mud can add more than 40 pounds to a bike if you don't take the right precautions.

Jumps

Catching air can be a blast, but make sure you know what the landing area is like beforehand. Off-road jumps can be especially treacherous; for all you know, you could be jumping off a cliff or into a giant bed of boulders.

Live Animals

Any time you're around live animals, pay close attention. Animals are unpredictable and always pose a threat.

Loam

Moist, slightly soft soil, otherwise known as loam, is one of the finest substances known to dirt bike riders. Traction is good, and the bike will rail through the corners and rocket out in a perfect drive. This near-perfect condition can lead to overconfidence, so be careful (but have fun).

Logs

Logs across the trail are a time-honored obstacle, one your ancestors were enduring long before you were a lecherous thought in your parents' minds. Techniques for crossing logs are found in the off-road section of this book. If the log looks like too much for your skills, stop and drag the bike over.

Mine Shafts

Mining onceflourished in some parts of the country, and abandoned mine shafts can still be found. If you're riding in an area that was known to be rich in gold or other minerals, look out for open mines. A good indication is a large mound of soil in the middle of nowhere.

Mud

Nothing is messier than mud, and its ability to trap riders is incredible. Mud robs momentum and ruins equipment. Mud gloms onto your bike in thick sheets and weighs it down. It ruins sprockets, chains, and brakes. When riding in mud, stiffen your suspension a bit, gear down a tooth or two, and ride a bit more conservatively.

The abrasive nature of mud will eat brake pads at an astounding rate. The most common way to combat this problem is to use solid brake rotors. Eliminating the standard holes used for cooling also does away with the most common way for mud to enter the brake caliper.

Rain

Moisture creates all sorts of problems, but usually its vision-ruining capabilities are what upset off-road motorcyclists the most. Also pay attention because rain quickly turns soil into mud, making it slippery.

Rain Ruts

Be alert for rain ruts at all times. If you get a wheel in one, it may be difficult to get it back out safely. If you do have to cross a rain rut, do so as perpendicularly as possible, and try to wheelie over it if conditions permit. This helps prevent the front wheel from getting stuck in its depths.

Roadkill

Treat dead animals on the trail like giant boulders. If you hit one, it could throw you over the handlebar or cause you to lose control of the steering. If you can't avoid one, get your weight back a bit and get on the throttle to lighten the front end.

Rocks

The density of rocks makes them something you should strive to avoid. If you hit one, it can and will cause great harm to man and machine. If you have to ride over a rock bed, stay alert and watch out for jagged edges that could puncture a tire.

Sand

Sand makes it tough to build and maintain momentum; therefore it has to be treated with respect. Try to stay away from deep sand whenever possible, because you may get stuck, which tends to overheat most engines.

Snow

Though it may appear harmless, a blanket of snow can hide rocks, tree roots, logs, branches, and other dangerous obstacles. Snow makes steering, accelerating, and braking difficult, especially when it's more than half a foot thick. Ice may also be underneath.

Trees

When riding around trees, the object is to avoid contact. Remember that most trees are immovable objects.

Tree Roots

The hardness of tree roots makes them particularly difficult obstacles to conquer,

especially if hidden. When riding around trees, keep an eye out for exposed roots, which will wreak havoc with steering and overall control.

Uphills

While most uphills pose little threat, watch out for variations in terrain that could produce a problem, especially loose terrain. If you're in sand with the throttle pinned and are producing a lot of wheelspin, then suddenly come upon a rock outcropping, you could be in serious trouble once the rear wheel gets traction.

Vines

Whether you encounter vines depends on the part of the country in which you ride. Vines can be tough to negotiate, since they want to rip you off your bike by your feet, hands, neck, and whatever else they can grab. While some vines actually break apart easily, others are quite strong (like steel cable) and will punish you if not taken seriously.

Water Crossings

When it's necessary to cross water, look

PRO SETUP TIPS
RIDING IN MUD

Mike Lafferty—"One of the best ways to keep your grips clean is protecting them with hand guards. They shield your hands and make the entire riding experience much more enjoyable."

Ricky Carmichael—"Tire choice is real important when it gets sloppy. Make sure you run tires designed for mud—otherwise, you'll struggle needlessly."

Ty Davis—"Mud will wear out chains and sprockets easily, so make sure you keep your chain properly adjusted. For that very reason, I recommend using an O-ring chain."

Rick Sowma—"Keep an eye on your master link. They seem to wear out easily in mud."

Steve Hatch—"Keep an eye on your radiators and make sure they're not getting covered in mud—otherwise, your bike could overheat."

Rick Sowma—"Spray all of your electrical connections with a water-displacing agent, and seal your ignition cover with silicone, so that water can't penetrate. It's also a good idea to put a zip tie around the base of the spark plug cap."

Ty Davis—"When it gets really wet and you're riding around rocks, you have to watch out for flat tires more than usual. Too much wheelspin with wet tires against rocks will usually cause tire failure pretty easily, so I usually run thicker inner tubes."

Rick Sowma—"I spray silicone spray under my fenders, so that mud doesn't collect."

Dick Burleson—"You always want to start every race with a clean bike. Mud can weigh down a bike, and that affects handling. It also hides parts that could be ready to fail or bolts that could be coming loose."

TERRAIN AND CONDITIONS

- Never ride faster than feels comfortable and safe.
- Always look ahead for upcoming obstacles and signs of danger.
- Always make sure you're traveling at a safe enough speed so you have plenty of room to apply the brakes in case you misread the terrain.
- Obstacles are more than rocks, jumps, trees, cacti, water, and so on. They also include other riders, cars, animals (both alive and dead), barbed wire, angry landowners, and anything else that could cause you harm.

for the area that appears the shallowest and narrowest. As a rule, don't cross any body of water unless you can see the bottom and/or see someone else do it and feel confident making an attempt. Water can be extremely harmful to your bike, especially if it gets sucked into your intake tract.

Wind

Wind makes it difficult to control a motorcycle, because you're always trying to overcompensate, especially in severe gusts. Reduce speeds or risk getting taken out by something you can't see.

Riding over downed trees can be difficult, but it often poses a fun challenge. This is eight-time National Enduro Champion Dick Burleson in Canada. *Ken Faught*

Chapter 4

BODY POSITION
The Starting Point

Many things will make you a better rider, but none is more important than developing a good understanding of basic riding position. This will lay the groundwork for all riding techniques and will eventually lead to your habits, both good and bad.

For starters, develop the correct body position and have it become natural. With practice and discipline, your body will automatically slip into the correct position. The more of a habit correct body position becomes, the better your riding will be. It's that simple.

Body positioning is always changing with terrain, conditions, and speed. By learning to move your body properly, you'll find obstacles passing easily and will use energy more efficiently. Amateur riders typically marvel at how long more advanced riders can race. Part of this comes from conditioning, but proper body position and efficient energy use are the reasons top riders can finish a rugged 20-minute moto or a grueling 6-hour off-road race and be fresher than an amateur in a 5-minute moto or 1-hour enduro.

Ever notice how the winning rider often has more energy left than those behind him? Jeremy McGrath and Chad Reed are two classic examples of this and are two of most relaxed and natural riders the sport has ever seen. A key to Jeremy's and Chad's speed is their body positioning, which is nearly flawless. When you're in the right place on the bike, everything else comes more easily.

The basic body position is similar for off-road riders, as Chad Reed demonstrates. Your knee should be directly above the footpeg, with your weight carried on the pegs and your upper body relaxed. Note how Chad carries his weight naturally and appears relaxed and comfortable while holding good body position.

The basic body position is to have your weight centered on the seat, with both feet on the footpegs, so you can make contact with the shift lever and brake pedal. Both hands should be on the controls, with one or two fingers on the clutch and brake levers, and your elbows up. You should be overgripping the throttle. Gary Semics calls this the central location.

The central location puts you at the center of the motorcycle and leaves you ready for whatever comes. By raising your elbows high, your arms have some built-in flex and

Sebastien Tortelli is in the attack position—the basic body position for most riding techniques—as he tackles this 90-foot tabletop. It starts with body weight centered, back arched slightly forward, knees bent, both feet on the pegs, elbows up, eyes looking ahead.

Most riders have at least one finger on the clutch at all times, as Dick Burleson shows in this tricky water crossing. Depending on the difficulty of clutch pull and your own style, you may end up using two fingers, but you'll have a better grip on the bars if you can train yourself to use one. The same goes for the front brake. *Ken Faught*

BODY POSITION

- Your head should be above the handlebar mounts (most of the time).
- Your knees should be bent, carrying your weight.
- Keep your elbows high.
- Overgrip the throttle.
- Have one or two finger(s) on the clutch and front brake levers.
- Keep your head up, and look ahead at upcoming obstacles.

the proper leverage for cornering. Modern off-road bikes deliver power explosively and are capable of incredible acceleration. High elbows and a forward position make you able to cope with that blast of speed when you open it up.

Most often, you'll be standing in the central location. Your knees should be bent

slightly; they serve as additional suspension for your weight. Most of your weight should be held in your legs, with your knees gripping the motorcycle. Your shoulders should be square and your upper body relaxed and supple.

Another key to the central location is that it allows you to make easy transitions on

the bike. By leaning forward or back, you can weight the front or rear.

The central location is usually effective in most instances, with a few modifications. Perhaps it's also preferred because it allows you to respond to shock quickly (as quickly as your reflexes allow), by enabling your knees, elbows, back, ankles, and wrists to absorb some of the shock. These same shock-absorbing characteristics are limited when you're sitting.

To improve your body position, start by putting the bike on the stand and carefully going through each of Gary Semics' techniques in this chapter. He describes exactly where you should be on the bike.

Once you're confident you have your body position correct, adjust your handlebars and control levers to suit. The more you change your body position, the more you'll have to fiddle with ergonomics to get the bike to fit.

Next, go out for a casual ride and focus on nothing but body position. Have a buddy watch you. Clue him in on what to look for and ask for his feedback. Better yet, have him make a videotape of you riding. You'll immediately see the areas where you need work.

Body position is the most basic skill for off-road riding. The concepts are reasonably simple, but mastering the technique takes years of practice. Keep refining your body position and you'll improve as a rider.

Gary Semics on Body Position

"When your desires are strong enough, you will appear to possess superhuman powers to achieve."

— **Napoleon Hill**

Body position is one of the most important factors in riding motocross. If your body is in the correct position, you and the motorcycle become a unit and will flow with the track. If you're out of position, things can go south in a hurry.

The fundamental aspect of body position is the central location, meaning you're at the center of the motorcycle. To master body position, the central location has to become automatic and natural. It will put you at the center of balance, a place where you can easily and naturally adjust your body to rapidly changing terrain. Maintaining the center of balance means your body positions and movements are always in the right place at the right time.

Mastering the use of all five controls deals with proper control of the clutch, throttle, front brake, rear brake, and shifter. When you have precise control of these elements, you have ultimate control over the motorcycle.

When twisting the throttle, it's usually best to use the wrist. This allows your elbow to stay up. Grab the bars tightly enough so you feel comfortable but not so tightly that you develop arm pump. If arm pump is a problem, it probably means you're gripping way too tight.

CENTER YOUR HEAD

When you're in the central location, sitting or standing, your head should be directly above the handlebar mounts.

This will position your body at the center of the motorcycle, right over the motorcycle's pivot point. If you move forward, you're in front of the pivot point. If you move back, you're behind the pivot point.

This is where all your body movements come from, and it's the center of your range of movement. Many beginning riders sit and stand with their body position too far back. This puts their weight behind the pivot point, causing the motorcycle to handle poorly. It also

Crouch your back to weight the front wheel. Your leg should be extended briefly in corners, to catch the bike if either wheel washes out. Mike Brown and his Team Pro Circuit Kawasaki demonstrate. *Ken Faught*

SITTING WEIGHT TRANSFER

When sitting, shift your weight by leaning your upper body rather than sliding on the seat.

Inexperienced riders often slide their butt back and forth on the seat to transfer weight. This is not the correct way to do it, unless it's an exception where you have to move far. The right way is to stay seated on the front part of the seat and lean your upper body back and forth. This simple technique transfers more weight to the rear or front of the motorcycle and allows your body position to remain at the center. This not only gives you better control, it's also much easier physically.

GO WITH THE FLOW

Relax your upper body enough to flow with the motorcycle.

Most inexperienced riders— and even some experienced riders—get this important technique wrong, especially when they're nervous. A common mistake is to carry tension in the upper body, mostly the arms and shoulders. This causes you and the motorcycle to be topheavy, because you'll support your weight on the handlebars. Your body will also be in the wrong position, because you can't flow with the motorcycle if you're tense and are supporting your weight on the handlebars.

The correct way to do it is to support your weight with your legs (on the footpegs) while your upper body is relaxed enough to flow with the motorcycle. This way, you can easily change body position and can be in the right place at the right time. Carrying your weight with your legs also lowers the center of gravity, so you and the motorcycle handle better.

The keys to riding motocross are balance, timing, and anticipating

causes arm pump, because the motorcycle is pulling hard on your arms when you accelerate. So, for the proper style, make sure you're doing this technique correctly and work from the center of the motorcycle.

KNEE POSITION

When you stand in the central location, your knee joint should be directly above your ankle joint. Squeeze the seat with your knees. When you move from this position, pivot from your knees where they squeeze the seat.

When you need to move further forward and back on the motorcycle while standing, move in a rowing motion while the insides of your knees slide along the sides of the

motorcycle. When you move from this position, you pivot from the footpegs.

A lot of beginning riders fail to squeeze the motorcycle with their knees, which causes a loose, separated feeling from the motorcycle. Push out a little with your feet on the footpegs as you pinch in with your knees. This technique keeps you from straining the insides of your legs. Make sure your footpegs are sharp, so your feet don't slip off.

When you need to move through your range of motion on the motorcycle, let your knees slide along the sides of the motorcycle, but still hold onto it with your legs.

When you've mastered these techniques, you'll notice more control, better endurance, and more of a connection to your iron horse."

Proper body position changes with every obstacle, especially when you're airborne. Mike LaRocco is in perfect position, with his elbows high and his head over the handlebar. Mastery of off-road riding requires learning to use all the controls smoothly—often several at once.

what's happening just before it happens. It's not in trying to force or hold things.

The first thing you need to relax is your mind. Be relaxed, clear, and ready for whatever comes up. Go with the flow."

LOWER YOUR CENTER OF GRAVITY

Carry most of your weight on the footpegs, to lower the center of gravity.

Carry your body weight on the footpegs first, the seat second, and the handlebars third. This maintains a low center of gravity in the center of the motorcycle. This technique is similar to Go with the Flow, but the focus is on the motorcycle instead of your body.

When you ride with a tense upper body, you're more likely to support your weight on the handlebars. This is the highest possible center of gravity the motorcycle has, and it's not a pivot point.

When the upper body is more relaxed, your body weight is carried on the footpegs. This lowers the motorcycle's center of gravity at the pivot point. When you can't support your weight on the footpegs (because the inside foot is out for a corner), support your weight on the seat and the outside footpeg. These are still pivot points, and they're at the center of the motorcycle.

Ride with a low center of gravity and use your legs to support your weight."

ELBOWS UP

Keep your elbows up and out, away from your sides, while overgripping the throttle.

Riders give up a lot of control if they grab the grips straight on and ride with their forearms parallel to the ground. They don't have the correct leverage between their upper body and the motorcycle. It's also more difficult to open the throttle.

High overgrip and high elbows enable you to use the full range of throttle in all body positions. This technique also gives you the correct leverage between your body and the motorcycle through your full range of movement.

Get used to this technique gradually, in a safe riding area. The throttle will feel a lot different with high overgrip, and it may be difficult to shut it off once you have that sucker wide open.

SQUARE SHOULDERS

Use side-to-side movement for control.

Your shoulders should move parallel across the motorcycle, from side to side. Don't twist your upper body. Keep your shoulders centered toward the direction you want to go.

You'll have more of a tendency to twist your upper body if you're riding with low elbows. The bad habit of twisting your upper body takes your body position out of the center of balance.

Keep your upper body centered toward the direction you want to go. Then move your body from side to side (parallel across the handlebars) to maintain balance and make the front wheel go exactly where you want it to. If your elbows are high, you have better leverage and this is much easier to do.

The fundamentals of motocross are balance, timing, and control. Your body has to move from the correct framework to develop this control. Through repetition, the position has to be ingrained into your nervous system until it becomes a reflex."

MOVE AROUND

In general, lean forward to accelerate and back to brake.

When you fail to do this correctly, you end up with your body weight in the wrong place at the wrong time. This can cause you to be out of control and make you work a lot harder than you need to.

Most of the time, when you accelerate, you need to lean forward into the force of acceleration. When you brake, you need to lean back against the force of braking. By moving your body, you maintain the center of balance. You and the motorcycle become one operating unit, and you can better maintain control.

Don't be a statue. Get used to moving on that motorcycle.

BACK POSITION

Straighten your back when leaning forward; crouch your back when moving back.

Riders commonly keep their backs in one position (always crouched or always straight). This is a bad habit, because it's more physically demanding. Back position should change according to body position on the motorcycle.

When you're in the forward body position, your back should be straight. This allows you to get up and over the front of the motorcycle. When you're in the back body position, your back

should be crouched. This allows you to lower your center of gravity and gives you better control. These are good techniques to practice frequently in a stationary position before trying them on the track.

Remember, there's more suspension on the motorcycle than the forks and shock. Use all of your body, including your back.

FOOT POSITION

Ride with the ball of your foot on the footpeg.

Some riders never ride with the balls of their feet on the footpegs. To see what category you fall into, check the wear marks on the bottoms of your boots. If you're one of these riders, you're missing out on the extra control you could be having.

A general rule is that if you're not using the shifter or brake, you should be on the balls of your feet. When you need to use the shifter or brake, move up to the arches of your feet, then move back to the balls of your feet when you're done. While riding, you're frequently changing back and forth. This is true whether sitting or standing.

The benefits to riding on the balls of your feet are that it adds another joint to your body's suspension (your ankle joint) for better movement and feel, your feet won't hit the ground in ruts and get ripped off the footpegs, and you won't hit the shifter or brake by accident.

This is definitely one of those techniques you have to think about and practice separately. Keep checking the bottoms of those boots.

FOOT POSITION WHILE BREAKING

When using the shifter or brake, the arch of your foot should be on the footpeg.

This is so you can reach the shifter and brake and operate them

correctly with the right leverage. Sometimes a rider might get it wrong, and his own feet get in the way. This can happen when you have the arches of your feet on the footpegs and you're not using the shifter or brake. What can get you into trouble is that you may hit the shifter or brake by mistake, which can knock the tranny into a false neutral (between gears) or throw you forward if you hit the rear brake unexpectedly. Either of these things could be minor mishaps or major traumas, depending on when they occur.

To avoid this, tilt your toes out, away from the shifter and brake, when you want to remain on the arches of your feet but don't want to use the shifter or brake. This is especially useful when you have too short a time between shifting and braking to move from your arches to the balls of your feet.

With practice and experience, you'll know just how far you need to tilt your toes out, and you'll notice if you happen to bump the shifter or brake by accident.

Feeling, timing, anticipation, and coordination in motocross add up to total flow concentration. This is one of the most rewarding sensations you can find. Many things may come close, but none of them can beat total flow concentration.

FOOT POSITION WHILE SHIFTING

When you're accelerating and your body is in the forward position, lift your foot off the footpeg to shift.

Most entry-level riders make the mistake of sliding their butt back on the seat to shift. This is so they can keep their foot on the footpeg and use the footpeg as a pivot point to lift the front of their foot up to shift. They're compromising their body position to shift.

When you're upshifting, your body position is usually forward, because you're accelerating. This means that to upshift, you have to lift your foot off the footpeg. This means you're using your whole leg to shift.

Keep that shift lever adjusted, so it's level with the top of the footpeg. If you adjust it too low, you're going to have a hard time reaching it to downshift and getting your foot under it to upshift, and you run the risk of the engine being knocked out of gear in a rut.

A good way to practice shifting is when you're working on your starts.

ONE OR TWO FINGERS ON THE CLUTCH

Use one or two fingers on the clutch, and keep those fingers on the clutch at all times.

This is an important technique, and it takes a lot of practice to master. The most common mistake is to hold onto the grip with all four fingers and then grab the clutch with all four fingers. This makes using the clutch awkward and, as a result, riders don't use the clutch often enough.

A pro rider has one or two fingers on the clutch lever 99 percent of the time. He uses it out of corners, through whoops, jumps, and certain kinds of bumps, to help deliver the exact amount of power to the rear wheel how and when he wants it.

The clutch should be used almost every time the throttle goes from closed to open, so if you want good controlled power, learn to use that low-end lever.

HAND DEXTERITY

Learn to work the levers and hold onto the grips independently.

The most common mistake is to hold onto the grips with all

Travis Preston is showing good form off a jump. He's forward from the attack position, with his elbows in and his head well over the front of the handlebar. His foot is positioned over the brake pedal, ready to stab it when needed.

four fingers, then grab at the levers only when you really have to use them. This way is so awkward that riders don't use the clutch and front brake levers often enough, and when they do use the levers, they can't hold onto the grips well.

It takes time and practice to develop the ability to hold the grips and work the levers accurately at the same time. Many riders use two fingers on the clutch; many use one finger. It's best to use one finger on the front brake. Get used to it and make it a habit.

Chapter 5

BRAKING
The Fine Art of Slowing Down

Braking may seem like one of the easiest tasks in the dynamic world of motorcycle riding, but in reality, it's one of the most difficult to perfect. Brake power, rider style, terrain, and line choice all factor into the equation. It's not as simple as grabbing a handful of front brake and standing on the rear brake pedal, but some general rules work in most situations.

Brakes can also be used for more than just slowing down. For example, they can help you hold a line in a turn, and tapping the rear brake while in the air will drop the front wheel.

Most of the brakes' stopping power comes from the front brake. When you're braking, the weight of the bike naturally transfers to the front wheel. With the rear wheel "light" (barely skimming the ground), the traction is all in the front wheel, and stopping power is in the front brakes. A bit of rear brake helps keep the bike straight and provides additional stopping power, but when you want to haul the bike down from warp nine to zero, the lever on the right side of the bars is where you'll find the most help.

Several products provide more powerful braking, and serious riders and racers experiment with the new technology. Items such as softer brake pads and 10–30mm oversized rotors can increase stopping power dramatically.

Body Position

For many reasons, body position is the most critical element of effective braking. Most braking is done while standing, with most rider weight toward the back of the bike, near the end of the seat or the beginning of the rear fender.

This additional weight on the rear end helps keep the back end of the bike on the ground and provides better control. The rider's rearward position also provides more leverage through the arms and legs, to keep the back end of the bike from coming around and swapping.

The key is to keep adjusting to terrain and conditions. There is no one set point for braking; you need to make subtle adjustments to keep the bike stable, with both wheels at least touching the ground.

"I find myself constantly moving my

Body position is always critical in braking. On this steep, high-speed downhill, Ricky Carmichael keeps his weight back and is applying the front brake with only one finger. Top riders use the one- and two-finger technique because hydraulic brakes don't require much pressure to activate.

1. These two sequences clearly show the effects braking bumps have on body positioning and suspension. Each sequence was shot in the same race, to create the most realistic comparison. This corner has two small bumps that most riders couldn't double. As Greg Albertyn enters the section, he's standing in the attack position but is hard on the brakes, as evidenced by the puff of dirt flying up from the rear wheel.

2. This aggressive approach requires Albee to shift his weight to the back of the bike. Experience has taught him that the back end will kick up as he rapidly decelerates and slams into the initial bump at race speed. He's using both brakes simultaneously, but he's cautious about using too much front brake, because it increases the likelihood of an endo as a result of the rear-wheel hop you'll see in the next few photos.

weight back and forth on the bike to achieve the desired body positioning while braking," claims multi-time AMA Supercross Champion Jeremy McGrath. "A couple inches either way makes a big difference."

Brake Straight

Most of your braking to slow the bike takes place in a straight line. When the bike is turning, heavy braking makes the tires slide, or push, through turns. This is what you want when brake-sliding the rear, but a front-wheel slide is harder to recover from. When you use the front brake too aggressively in a turn, the front wheel is prone to tucking under, which usually results in a low-side crash.

The most effective way to reduce the pushing effect is to apply less power to the front brake and/or steer with the throttle—that is, use the power of the motor to help you turn. This may seem like an odd technique, especially in a chapter devoted to braking. However, in some turns, such as chicanes

(tight corners inserted to slow the race down), the bike may handle better, because the effects of braking and applying the throttle will upset the suspension less.

The other common scenario when turning and braking at the same time occurs when the back end of the motorcycle can't slow down at the same rate as the front. In essence, the rear end's extra momentum makes it want to come around perpendicular to the track. In extreme cases, the bike can do a 180-degree spin. This is desirable for a brake-slide but can surprise you when the back end squirts out unexpectedly. If you're caught off guard, the back end can come around, catch, and pitch you off in a high-side crash.

Let's get back to braking a straight line. From a technical standpoint, the back end shouldn't come around on one side if the bike is in a perfectly straight line. Stated as simply as possible, the mass of the rear end should instead push the steering stem against the steering head, which in turn should put more weight on the front of the motorcycle. This is

precisely why a bike will endo (while braking in a straight line) when body positioning is incorrect or in instances of overbraking. Once again, this is the result of the rear wheel not being able to slow down the back end of the bike at the same rate as the front.

Though you may not like to hear that the front end of your bike can push at all speeds, or worse, endo, these problems can be reduced through proper braking. In most cases, both brakes should be applied evenly and progressively. You should begin braking early enough so that you have time to momentarily back off the brakes in case overbraking fouls up the handling.

Most of the time, brakes are used together. Using only the rear brake is useful for brake-sliding. The front is best used with a bit of rear brake, which helps keep the bike straight and provides more stopping power.

Brake-Slides

Brake-slides are a good way to turn quickly, although they rob momentum. They

3. As expected, Albertyn gets a big hop from the effects of his suspension reacting to the first bump under braking. This hop is due partially to the position of his fork and shock in the suspension stroke. Upon braking, the resistance causes both ends to collapse somewhat, which positions the suspension in a stiffer part of the stroke. To combat this "problem," Albertyn readjusts his weight, placing his butt over the rear fender, and stretches out his arms to simultaneously push the front end down.

4. Proper planning allows Albee to maintain control and enter the corner in the line he's chosen. Maintaining full control is essential for effective braking.

work better in flat turns, but good riders learn to do them on most any camber. The principle is no different from the one you probably used to slide your bicycle around. Pull in the clutch, lock the rear brake, and gently turn the motorcycle right or left. The rear will shoot out, and the back end will swing around. The key to making a brake-slide useful is to coordinate the brake and throttle, so that you go in doing a brake slide and come out in controlled power slide. This takes a lot of practice, and you should start cautiously. Work in an open, flat area if possible, and try it at low speeds. Once you get it down, a brake-slide is a great way to pass someone on the inside.

When using the rear brakes, it's usually necessary to pull in the clutch, especially at slower speeds, to make sure your engine doesn't stall if the rear wheel locks up. For the same reason, you may have to rev your engine while braking if your bike doesn't idle.

One of the most important points to remember is that brakes are effective only when the wheels are touching the ground. Avoid landing off jumps with the brakes applied, because this dramatically changes the way the bike handles. The suspension usually won't respond well, and it increases the odds of the tires sliding out.

Elevation Braking

Braking technique changes on slopes. When traveling downhill, you have to adjust your body position to keep some weight on the rear wheel. Aggressive use of the front brake on a downhill weights the front end to a larger degree than on level parts of the track. This can be compensated for by moving your body back a bit farther, but it's a problem when the terrain is rough. If you're braking aggressively, the front suspension will be loaded with most of your and the bike's weight. If you hit a big braking bump, the suspension will probably bottom and the bike may endo, pitching you over the bars. To avoid this, plan your braking carefully on a downhill, so you can release or

brake lightly over braking bumps or similar obstacles.

Downhills also require earlier braking, because it's much more difficult to brush off momentum. If you find you're going too fast and don't feel comfortable applying the front brake, you can attempt to traverse the hill with a technique much like the one skiers use to slow down.

Braking while traveling uphill is much easier, because the weight of the bike and rider is naturally carried to the rear, and the forces of gravity make it easy to brush off speed. For these reasons, you'll probably find you can brake much later than you normally could on level ground.

Slippery Conditions and Off-Cambers

Traction also plays an important role in deceleration. In most situations, the goal should be a line that offers the most grip. When possible, avoid sand, mud, or other slick

5. Since Albertyn maintains the attack position, he's able to "blip" the throttle as the rear wheel comes in contact with the second bump, and he avoids a small hole that's been created on the other side. This allows the suspension to settle, and now Albee's in good position to execute a turn.

BRAKING

- **Body position is crucial. Most braking is done in the standing position, with knees bent, elbows up, and weight back a bit.**
- **Adjust body position to keep the rear wheel on the ground.**
- **Complete most of your braking before initiating a turn.**
- **Apply the brakes progressively.**
- **Avoid locking up the front wheel.**
- **When possible, choose lines that avoid sand, mud, or braking bumps.**
- **Brake before or after braking bumps.**
- **Apply the brakes gently on slippery surfaces such as sand, mud, snow, or ice.**

surfaces. If you have to brake when traction is poor, use the brake more gently and progressively. Similarly, avoid overly aggressive braking on off-cambers. Off-cambers allow fewer tire treads to grip, and only those on one side of the tire, which allows the front end of the bike to twist and slide out. Because tires are prone to locking up more easily on slippery surfaces, braking must be done with finesse and less power.

"I rarely use the front brake in deep sand," says 1995–96 AMA 125cc National Motocross Champion Steve Lamson. "I notice that the front wheel tends to dig in and causes the back end of the bike to swap. When I do use the front brake in sand, I apply it very slowly and don't use much force."

It's also important to analyze braking bumps carefully. When possible, stay clear of them. Braking bumps make it tough to brush off speed quickly, because they make the suspension more active. Braking bumps also tire riders and induce arm pump more easily than most other obstacles. You may want to get most of your braking done before or after crossing braking bumps, so you can let off the brakes and let the suspension work over the bumps.

Uphill Braking

Gravity makes it easier to stop on an incline, but it also affects suspension. The quicker deceleration forces the suspension to dive, which can hinder handling, especially if you're in a section of braking bumps.

Braking Bumps Part 2

1. Doug Henry finds a creative line around the same obstacle. This is one of the rewards of riding the edges of the track and continuing to look at the changing lines. Here he rides around the outside of the jump and doesn't upset his suspension.

2. Because he's not worried about making major body changes, Henry's able to drive into the turn much harder than Albertyn and set up for the turn much sooner. At this point he already has his foot out, ready to make the left-hand turn.

3. Henry's just about finished with braking and makes final preparations to enter the turn. A split second later he's off the brakes and back on the throttle. Also note that he uses much less energy in this section and maintains more control the entire time.

Gary Semics on Braking

"Confidence doesn't come from nowhere. It's a result of something—hours and days and weeks and years of constant work and dedication."

— Roger Staubach

Front Brake

The brakes do more than slow the motorcycle down. Used properly, they add precision to your control of the machine. Begin with proper foot and hand position and move on to these advanced techniques.

Remember that if you aren't braking or accelerating, you're going to get passed.

Many riders use the front brake to help settle into corners, as shown by Jimmy Button. He uses a little front brake to make sure the front end doesn't run away from him as he negotiates this section, which is slightly off-camber.

REAR BRAKING WHILE STANDING

When standing, pivot the arch of your foot on the footpeg and depress the rear brake pedal with the ball of your foot.

Some riders have different parts of their foot on the footpeg when using the rear brake. Sometimes they're on the arch, sometimes they're on the heel. They fail to develop the proper habit and the feeling of controlling the rear brake.

When you're standing while using the rear brake, always have the footpeg in the arch of your foot, right in front of the heel. Then your foot can pivot on the footpeg and give you the same good feel of the rear brake every time. Find the control.

REAR BRAKING WHILE SITTING

When sitting, lift your foot off the footpeg and depress the rear brake pedal with the ball of your foot.

As you hold your braking leg up, keep that leg tight against the side of the motorcycle. As soon as you finish with the rear brake, put your foot back on the footpeg.

Most beginning riders get all mixed up while braking, either standing or sitting. This is because there's one braking technique for standing (which we just covered) and a different one for sitting.

Some riders try to keep their foot on the footpeg and use the rear brake while sitting. This won't work while sitting on the front of the seat, because your foot and ankle just won't bend that far. Some riders use their heel on the rear brake while sitting, which isn't good either.

If you watch a pro, you'll see he lifts his foot up off the footpeg, locks his leg in place against the side of the motorcycle, and uses the ball of his foot on the rear brake by flexing his ankle. This technique gives you the most control.

Practice this with the bike on the stand at first, then while the bike is moving.

REAR BRAKING DURING TRANSITION

To control the rear brake through the transition from standing to sitting, lift your right foot as you sit and shift your weight to the left footpeg.

Wouldn't it be terrible if every time you went from standing to sitting, you had to let go of the rear brake or you couldn't control the rear brake anymore? Just because you're going from standing to sitting doesn't mean you don't need the rear brake. In fact, that just might happen to be the place where you need it the most.

We just covered how to use the rear brake while standing and while sitting. You must also have control between standing and sitting. As you begin to sit down for the corner, lift your right foot up off the footpeg and still control the rear brake. This means your weight has to shift to the left footpeg until you get your weight to the front part of the seat. Then, as you're sitting on the front part of the seat, lock your leg against the side of the motorcycle and hold your leg above the rear brake as you use it with the ball of your foot.

Practice this with the bike on the stand at first, then while the bike is moving.

CLUTCH OUT WHILE BRAKING

When braking into a corner, downshift and leave the clutch out. Let the back pressure of the engine help slow you down. This is like an anti-lock system. While braking, pull the clutch in only

Small Braking Bumps

1. Greg Albertyn approaches this section once again in the attack position and can be more aggressive than in his previous sequence.

2. Albee's once again experiencing some rear wheel hop, but this time it's less noticeable. Again he repositions his body weight, placing his butt over the rear fender, and extends his arms to push the front end down. Notice how much abuse the fork takes under these circumstances.

when you want to lock up the rear wheel.

The wrong techniques in braking cause you to lose time and could even get you into trouble. When a rider comes into a corner carrying too much speed for his ability to slow down, you'll see him doing all kinds of panic braking, from locking up the rear wheel at 40 miles per hour to freewheeling and back to sliding again.

The proper way is good, steady, controlled braking. Start off with hard braking and then progressively lighter and lighter braking as you enter the corner. This technique works far better if you leave the clutch out as you brake and downshift for the corner (don't use the clutch to downshift). This way, the engine helps slow you down and produces a steadier braking effect. The rear wheel has the best braking effect just before it locks up.

If you can't do this technique well, practice your control of the rear brake lever.

3. At this point, another interesting situation occurs. The line leading into the corner starts to bend, and Albertyn is forced to back off slightly on the front brake.

DOWNSHIFT WITHOUT THE CLUTCH

You don't need the clutch when you downshift.

Some inexperienced riders use the clutch to downshift and then just hold it in while they brake the rest of the way into the corner. Using the clutch to downshift is not necessary. By leaving the clutch out while braking, the engine's back

4. Albertyn almost throws it away here. He's been overly aggressive with the front end, and his tire has started to plow (notice the roost coming off the front wheel). He completely lets go of the front brake and tries to stand the bike straight up, to avoid crashing.

pressure will make your braking smooth and steady.

It is necessary to use the clutch when you upshift, because the transmission has torque on the gears from the power of the engine. But the gears are under little torque when the throttle is off and you're slowing down. So leave that low-end lever (the clutch) out when you're downshifting and braking for a corner.

DRAG THE REAR BRAKE OVER OBSTACLES

Dragging the rear brake reduces the rear wheel's tendency to kick up on certain bumps and obstacles.

When a beginning rider gets into trouble, such as having the rear wheel kick up too high, he usually just freezes and waits to see what happens. One thing you can do to avoid this kicking-up effect is to drag the rear brake when you think the rear wheel is going to kick up. This puts a little down-force on the rear suspension and greatly reduces rear-wheel kick.

The next time you see that you're going to hit a big bump or a whoop harder than you want to, touch or drag that rear brake and see how much it holds the rear end down. I know it's saved me from an endo many times.

This is another good reason to be able to use the rear brake from any body position on the motorcycle—because in this case, you'll be standing with your weight back.

5. Quick thinking allows Albee to save it. He finishes up his braking with the rear brake and remains in the attack position the entire time.

Braking Seated

In low-speed corners that don't have any braking bumps, it's fairly common for riders to do all their braking while seated. The low speed and lowered center of gravity reduce the risk of an endo. Typically, both the front and rear brakes are applied evenly.

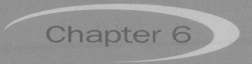

Chapter 6

ACCELERATION
More Than Just a Handful of Throttle

Acceleration is one of the most critical aspects in all of motorcycling, and the reason is simple: the harder you accelerate, the faster you go. Getting a clean drive can be the key to everything from a clean setup for a pass to clearing a big jump.

However, acceleration is more than just grabbing a handful of throttle and unleashing all the ponies in your stable. Accelerating correctly is a blend of proper body position, throttle control, clutch use, and line choice. Sound familiar?

Before you can think about line choice, you have to have a goal with the acceleration. Most of the time, riders strive for the shortest route, because it's presumably quicker—but imagine if you're tackling a nasty uphill or attempting a supercross-style triple jump. In these situations, it may be necessary to get a better run at the obstacle, to increase speed and momentum. Therefore, look at each situation carefully.

"Try to maintain momentum as best as possible," says Steve Lamson. "It's much easier to accelerate when you've already got speed. If you come to a complete stop, your

A good drive out of a corner can set you up for a pass, cut down your lap times, or just feel great. The key is getting the rear wheel hooked up and keeping the bike straight. Ricky Carmichael does both in fine fashion and weights the front end by leaning forward.

Momentum

One way to get a better drive is to choose lines that allow you to carry more speed through the corner. Mike Brown and his Pro Circuit Kawasaki demonstrate.

Acceleration Bumps

Putting power to the ground is sometimes a difficult task, especially in uneven terrain. When acceleration bumps become too large, it's necessary to stand, as James Dobb does while exiting this turn. *Joe Bonnello*

bike has to work harder, and you'll have a difficult time getting traction."

It's much more efficient to accelerate in a straight line than while turning, because your bike has less resistance, and the tire has more contact surface with the ground.

Terrain determines the difficulty of acceleration. In loam, where traction is abundant, acceleration will be relatively easy, but you have to fight the bike's natural tendency to wheelie. In sharp contrast, it's a battle to find traction on dry hardpack or in sand (either shallow and deep). As a result, it's easy to break the rear wheel loose and lose control.

Regardless of terrain type, the quest for traction (which leads to acceleration) involves a series of body repositionings, to keep both wheels on the ground. Ideally, you want to keep as much weight on the rear wheel as possible, so it will stay in constant contact with the ground, but you also need to avoid wheelying. If a bike starts to wheelie, most likely it will lose speed. If you're not prepared, you could chop the throttle, reducing your drive.

"To reduce the chances of wheelying, place your body weight over the front of the bike," instructs Steve Lamson. "One of the exceptions would be downhills, where most of the time you would want to stand with your weight towards the back of the bike."

Fresh tires are also important. "To get the best acceleration, you must have good tires, preferably new ones that are designed for the terrain," says Lamson. "Otherwise, you'll get too much wheelspin, and it will be impossible to get the best drive."

Another hindrance to acceleration is called an acceleration bump. These obstacles, usually found in series and ranging up to a foot or so tall, foul up suspension and make acceleration difficult. In this situation, search for an alternative line that provides a smoother route, although one may not always be available. When forced to negotiate acceleration bumps, the best way is to let your knees and elbows work with the suspension, to keep it on the ground as much as possible. You can also traverse these obstacles a gear higher than usual. This will lessen the torque effect of the chain and allow the rear suspension to soak up the bumps and keep the back tire on the ground. The engine won't be shrieking at peak rpm, but your drive will be stronger and smoother.

Controlling Wheelies

Weight the front end to keep the bike from wheelying. Notice how Jimmy Button has his upper torso over the fuel tank and handlebar. If the front end comes up too much, slip the clutch ever so slightly to drop the front wheel without destroying the drive.

Changing Lines

1. Mike LaRocco decides that the rut used by other riders has gotten too deep to use effectively. Instead, he slows his entrance speed and cuts the corner more sharply.

ACCELERATION

- Select the gear that will allow the engine to work the most efficiently.
- Avoid wheelspin through careful throttle control and clutch use.
- Search for lines that offer the most traction.
- Use your legs to absorb acceleration bumps while standing.
- Try to carry as much momentum as possible.
- Adjust your weight forward and backward to find the delicate balance that gives the rear wheel traction without allowing the bike to wheelie.
- Acceleration is most effective in a straight line.

"If there are a lot of acceleration bumps, you may want to try to wheelie over them," says Jeremy McGrath. "Try to get your front wheel to skim over the top of them, so that your front suspension won't be affected. This will allow the shock to do its job and keep the rear wheel on the ground as much as possible."

McGrath's approach is aggressive and requires precise throttle control to make sure the front wheel doesn't rise too quickly and cause the rider to lose control. At times, however, you may consider slowing down, to actually speed your travel.

"Sometimes, in order to accelerate the hardest, you have to be patient," says Ron Lechien. "In some cases, if you get on the throttle too hard too soon, you can make mistakes that will cost you time. To prevent

2. Since LaRocco reduced his speed more than normal to hug the inside of the turn, it's much easier to lose traction under hard acceleration. As you can see, he's already starting to get sideways as he drives out of the turn.

this, practice rolling on the throttle without using the clutch. This will also help you determine which gear works best, but it will help make you a smoother rider. And if you can be smooth and make few mistakes, usually you'll become faster."

Lechien also points out that gearing can make a big difference in the drive you get out of the corners. "Make sure your bike is geared correctly for your type of riding, otherwise acceleration will be hindered," Lechien says.

Ideally, you should be able to come out of a corner and get a good drive by rolling the throttle open, with perhaps a quick stab at the clutch. If you find that several corners require excessive clutch abuse in one gear, while in another gear you exit and immediately overrev, try changing the final gearing. A tooth or two less on the rear sprocket is great for subtle changes, while changing the gearing on the front sprocket will provide larger changes.

3. LaRocco becomes too aggressive and is forced to get out of the throttle to straighten up the bike. Had he continued to stay on the gas, he probably would have slid out and been tossed off the high side.

Gary Semics on Acceleration

"Concentrate, put all your eggs in one basket, and watch that basket."
— Andrew Carnegie

The throttle should be used for much more than just speeding up. A bit of power to the rear wheel can place the front wheel and is key to jumping and whoops. With modern off-road motorcycles, the fundamental skill of using the throttle is moderation. Your bike is a powerful, explosive weapon. Learn to use that power precisely, like a surgeon with a scalpel.

Once again, you should be either on the gas or on the brakes. Don't coast.

Smooth Power

Getting the tire hooked up requires coordinated use of the clutch and throttle. When traction is good, be careful not to use too much throttle and cause a wheelie. When traction is poor, it's a trick to get the tire hooked up at all. In most cases, smooth application of power is key. Mike LaRocco has fine form here—his body is over the handlebars, weighting the front end, and his left foot is in position, ready to shift up.

USE THE CLUTCH

Whenever you accelerate hard, use the clutch and throttle together.

When many beginning riders want to accelerate hard, they simply open the throttle and wait for the engine to build rpm to reach the meat of the powerband. Once in a while they might get lucky and just happen to be near the powerband, but if they're too far below it, they won't get the power they want when they need it.

Of course, you need to be in the right gear for the amount of speed and momentum you're carrying. Don't slip the clutch too much. In this case, the clutch is just a helper, not a means. When this technique is done correctly, you can use more of the engine's power. This is because you can begin to accelerate from the bottom of the powerband instead of starting from the middle or near the top.

By using the clutch and throttle together, you cause the engine to build the right amount of rpm just how and when you want it. By slipping the clutch a little, the engine will come in on the powerband. If you use just the throttle, the engine may bog and hesitate before it can reach the powerband.

On fast areas it may be necessary to stand up to get the best drive. Here, Brian Swink is able to absorb some of the acceleration bumps with his knees, thus helping the suspension keep the rear wheel hooked up.

Water & Rocks

You have to be careful when accelerating in streambeds, as *Dirt Rider* editor-in-chief Ken Faught does here. It's difficult to tell what's beneath the surface, and it can spell disaster if you get overly aggressive.

FRONT WHEEL PLACEMENT

Use the clutch and throttle as you pull up on the handlebars, to carry the front wheel a little farther down the track and set it down where you want. This is called front wheel placement.

The common mistake is to just let the front wheel bounce, hit, and land wherever it may, by chance. If you do this, you're going to be in for a rough ride, and you'll have to slow down to compensate for it. Pro riders have the ability to lift, carry, and set the front wheel down wherever they want, to miss bumps and land in G-out troughs to smooth things out.

Of course, you need to pull back on the bars and maintain the correct body positions, but the other half is accomplished with the clutch and throttle. Use the clutch and throttle together to deliver just the right amount of power to the rear wheel, so you can carry the front wheel to where you want to place it.

Chapter 7

CORNERING
A Look at the World of Turns

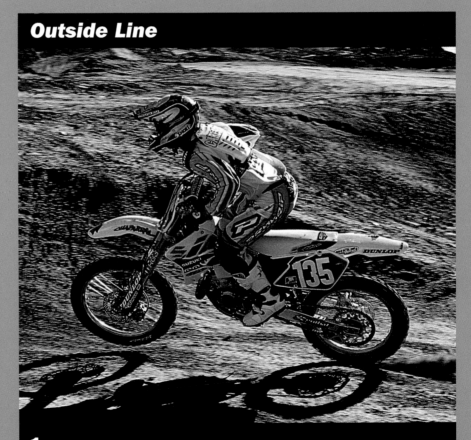

Outside Line

1. This banked turn offers a variety of lines. On the inside is a rut, in the middle it's smooth, and on the outside is a small berm. Danny Carlson determines that in this case, the outside is the faster line. Because a kicker jump leads into the turn, Carlson is still in the standing position and is finishing his braking while trying to go as straight as possible.

Many variables determine how fast a motorcycle can be turned: speed, available traction, terrain type, amount of turning, body positioning, and throttle control. Of those ingredients, you usually have control only over the latter two, yet paired, they encompass thousands of combinations that make cornering very, very challenging.

While cornering doesn't offer the thrill of jumping, cliff climbing, or some of the airborne aspects of the sport, it's probably the most common obstacle you'll encounter. It's also the best place on the track to pass. For this simple reason, spend a fair amount of time working on your cornering technique, especially if racing is on your agenda.

Good technique starts with body positioning designed to lower the center of gravity and maintain traction at both wheels. In most cases, this means sitting down, shifting your weight to the most forward portion of your seat, sticking your inside leg out, and applying pressure to the outside footpeg. Combined with cautious throttle application, to make sure the front end doesn't come off the ground and the rear wheel doesn't slide out, this is the foundation for developing good cornering habits.

Even though you're sitting most of the time, it's also important to be able to absorb some of the bumps with your knees and elbows. Usually, you want to stay relaxed in the turns, so you can help the suspension soak up

James Stewart is known for his aggressive riding style, as this shot perfectly illustrates. Even though he saves it, he does a lot of things wrong to put himself in this awkward position. Many of the top pros insist that sometimes it's best to actually slow down to shave seconds off your lap times. *Massimo Melani*

2. In a split second, Carlson shifts his body position and begins the turn using the banking for traction-inducing resistance. Furthermore, he's looking for a point to start his turn.

3. As Carlson reaches the apex of the turn, he decides the berm might not be that strong, so he decides to brake-slide into the banking. He pulls the clutch in, backs off slightly on the front brake, and leans into the turn just as he stands on the rear brake. This locks up the rear wheel for a split second. This lets his bike slide sideways in a controlled manner and allows him to get his RM125 pointed in the right direction for his exit. Notice how he keeps his inside leg out—in case a wheel slips out—until he has the bike aimed straight. Also, throughout the entire turn he weights the outside footpeg, to produce better traction to both wheels.

whatever changes in the terrain come your way. If you're rigid, your bike will get bounced all over the place, and if your wheels break contact with the ground, you increase your chances of falling.

Ready to Dab

Because leaning into a turn can feel awkward, most riders find it natural to put out a leg in case a small dab is required. "When you stick your leg out, you've got to make sure you keep it in front of your body," says Jeremy McGrath. "It won't do you any good if it slides back, because you won't have any leverage to support your weight."

"When you stick your leg out, make sure your toes are pointed up," says Ron Lechien. "This way, if your boot catches on something, it should deflect off the sole instead of causing your foot to get bent back."

Like all techniques, this has many variations you'll find helpful. In high-speed sections, you may find it necessary to stand, especially if the areas are too rough for your suspension to handle with you seated. When you stand through a turn, you still try to weight the front of the motorcycle, to make sure the front wheel has traction—but keep both feet on the footpegs. This way you can control your balance better, and you can use both knees to absorb changes in the terrain.

Gear Selection

Regardless of whether you're sitting or standing, many riders agree it's best to pick one gear and stick with it until you're out of the turn. "Usually, I try not to shift in a corner," says Danny Carlson. "I make sure my bike is in the correct gear when I enter the turn, because it saves time, and it's much smoother. The only time I find I'm forced to shift mid-turn is at the exit around big sweepers, where my bike would normally tend to overrev. When the bike overrevs, the power falls off pretty abruptly, and it slows your drive."

Another important aspect is line choice in the turn. "Try to make your arch smooth," says Jeremy McGrath. "Any quick movements will cause you to lose traction easier. That's why you also want to roll on the throttle and stay off the clutch as much as possible. It's always difficult trying to figure out just how hard you can get on the gas."

"If there's a banking around the outside, you may want to use it, because it'll give you

4. Though Carlson is leaning his bike over, he keeps his body almost perfectly straight up and down to help maintain traction. As he exits the turn, he's on the gas and is using the clutch to build power on his small two-stroke.

5. Even as Carlson exits, he keeps his inside foot out for balance and weights the outside footpeg for traction. You can see he's starting to return his inside foot to the peg and is already under full throttle.

6. The final product is a mistake-free arch as Carlson powers to the next obstacle.

more traction than a flat turn," adds Lechien. "Also look for any good ruts. If you find a good rut that you can rail, you can get on the gas harder and turn quicker."

Bermed (or banked) corners can be helpful, because they offer a lot more resistance for your tires and usually decrease the chances of losing traction. Unfortunately, most berms are located at the outermost edges of turns, forcing you to take the long route, which can be slower than a more risky inside line. Ultimately, you have to determine which is better.

Ruts

In contrast, most ruts develop first at the inside of turns. When used properly, ruts can be the express way around a turn, but they can also be hazardous. The most common problem occurs when a rider is too aggressive, carries too much momentum into a rutted turn, and can't get both wheels firmly seated into the groove.

The idea with rutted turns is to line up with the rut prior to the entrance, so both wheels drive in naturally. If one wheel doesn't line up, you have an increased chance of falling.

Once both wheels are in the rut, it's important to maintain momentum. In most cases, this requires moderate throttle application. You don't want to accelerate too hard, or you could cause the bike to wheelie and the front wheel to jump out of the rut, which is another no-no that can get you in trouble.

You also want to keep an eye on the depth of the ruts you choose. If they get too deep, you could get stuck, because the rut walls will start grabbing your chain guide, axles, and lower fork tubes. If you feel that a rut is getting dangerously deep, look for an alternative line; odds are that one is just a few feet away.

Line Selection

Regardless of whether you're turning on the flat or using a berm or rut to assist you in your search for traction, it's always best to experiment with as many lines as possible, to see what works best.

"Look for the smoothest line around the corner that will offer you the best traction," says Steve Lamson. "Stay away from bumps, if you can, and watch for mud or other things that could be slippery. Also, if you find that you have to cross ruts in a turn, it's best to cross them

Inside Lines

1. This is the same turn on which you saw Lamson rail the outside earlier, except this time he's snagging the inside line. The line is difficult to get to because of a small double jump immediately before the corner. To brush off speed more quickly, Lamson lands short, to use the second jump for resistance.

2. Lamson finishes his braking and lines his bike up with the rut. The idea is to enter the rut as straight as possible, so both wheels line up perfectly.

3. Lamson goes from standing to sitting in one quick motion, then drops his inside leg for balance. His weight is on the frontmost portion of the seat, which helps load the front suspension and eventually helps provide more traction to the front tire.

4. As the rear wheel rolls into the groove, Lamson prepares to roll on the throttle. Throttle application must not be too aggressive, or the rear wheel may jump out of the rut.

CORNERING

- **Most cornering is done in the seated position, to lower the center of gravity.**
- **Weight the front of the bike, to help the front wheel maintain traction.**
- **Train yourself to roll the throttle on when exiting corners, which allows you to smooth and start your drive earlier.**
- **Do most of your braking before initiating the turn.**
- **When possible, try to make wide, gradual turns, to maintain momentum.**
- **Look for berms and ruts that could help you turn more quickly, especially on off-camber turns.**
- **Try an assortment of lines.**

as perpendicular as possible, so they don't catch the sidewalls of your tires and cause you to lose control. Even if you don't crash, it'll waste time and energy. You also want to avoid rocks or anything else that could cause either one of your wheels to break loose. If you hit something with your bike leaned over, it'll be difficult to maintain control."

It's also critical to avoid hard braking in any turn, unless you have to avoid a downed rider or something else dangerous. Jamming on the brakes will cause your wheels to slide, especially when you're leaned over, and if you are, the natural tendency is to straighten your bike and force it to go straight.

"Do all of your braking before the turn," says Mike Craig. "Most bikes turn better with the throttle on. If you brake in the turn, it may cause the bike to stand straight up."

5. Lamson gets back on the throttle. His weight is still forward, his inside foot is out with the toes angled up, and both elbows are up.

6. As he exits the turn, Lamson starts accelerating harder but keeps the same body positioning. Had there been acceleration bumps, he might have tried to wheelie them by sliding some of his weight back on the seat. It wouldn't be a true wheelie—just high enough for the front wheel to skim over the tops of the initial bumps, so it wouldn't hamper steering.

7. The final stages of the turn show Lamson beginning to retract his foot and replace it on the footpeg.

Be sure and try several different lines through a turn. Even if one is the fastest, you may find you'll need to take a different one to pass or avoid a downed rider or that a different line becomes faster as the track gets worn down.

All handling characteristics change with the type of terrain and the type of traction. On slippery surfaces, such as hardpack and mud, you have to be less aggressive with both body position and throttle application. You can usually be more aggressive when it comes to riding in loam or sand.

Gary Semics on Cornering

"The mind is the limit. As long as the mind can envision the fact that you can do something, you can do it, as long as you believe 100 percent."

— Arnold Schwarzenegger

The fundamental skills in cornering are body position and coordinating the brakes and throttle. Use the brakes up until the point you get back on the throttle, feathering each during the transition. Using the brakes will also help you hold a line.

Remember, never coast. Brake or accelerate at all times, and occasionally do both.

Brake to Turn

1. This reverse-angle sequence of Lamson taking the same inside line shows brake-sliding and how using both brakes helps cornering. In this shot, Lamson is hard on both brakes. Although his body position is forward, his torso is straight, keeping some weight on the rear tire. He lifts his heel off the right peg, to use the rear brake effectively while sitting.

OUTSIDE ELBOW UP

Raise your outside elbow above the handlebar when cornering. Your inside elbow should be a little lower.

If your outside elbow drops or is low while cornering, you'll have a tendency to twist your upper body toward the outside of the turn. This will prevent you from having proper leverage and move your body out of the center of balance.

To perform this technique correctly, overgrip the outside grip, so you can keep your outside elbow up high above the handlebar. Your inside elbow should be in a neutral position that feels comfortable. Keep your shoulders facing the direction you want to go and work your upper body from this framework, to control the motorcycle and maintain the center of balance.

Stay at the center of balance and work the bike from there. Slide the bike and make it do what you want it to. Don't try to lean and twist your body to the outside or hold the bike in position.

INSIDE FOOT OUT

When cornering, put your inside foot out in front of you, very lightly sliding on the ground and ready to lift the motorcycle up straighter if it tries to lean over too far. While doing this, keep some pressure on the outside footpeg.

The position in which you hold your inside foot while going through a corner is important. The common mistakes are to use the inside foot for a counterbalance and not to be able to use it to lift the motorcycle if it tries to lean over too far or slide out. The common mistake with the

2. Lamson has the rear wheel locked up and initiates a brake-slide to turn the motorcycle. His outside elbow is up, and his shoulders are square to the bike. The front wheel is turned slightly left, anticipating the rear-wheel slide. It also appears that he applies light pressure to the front brake, which holds the front end to a tighter line.

outside foot Is to have the arch of the foot (rather than the ball) on the footpeg and to just let it rest on the footpeg instead of pushing down on it.

To do this correctly, your inside foot should be just barely skimming the ground. It should be in a position to give you a good shot at lifting the motorcycle if the front wheel slides out. You don't want your hip, knee, and ankle to be locked, but you do need to have them stiff enough to hold the proper position. When you don't need that inside foot out there anymore, get it back on the footpeg as soon as possible.

While you're doing this, keep some pressure on the outside footpeg to maintain a low center of gravity, especially in flat corners without a berm. Practice this technique separately to develop your reflexes.

INSIDE FOOT TIMING

Put your inside foot out for the part of the turn where you're going from braking to accelerating (exit dex) and get it back on the footpeg as soon as possible.

The common mistake is to put the foot out for the turn too early. Many riders do this to help with balance, making the mistake of using their leg as a counterbalance. If you keep your shoulders square and your body centered, you don't need the leg as a counterbalance.

After making the corner, many riders keep their foot off the peg too long. This puts their weight on the seat, which makes those accelerating bumps beat their ass.

The correct way to do this is to put your foot out for the least amount of time possible. The foot should be out in the part of the turn where you're switching from braking to accelerating. I call this part of the turn the exit dex. Your foot should come out for this part of the turn and then get back on the footpeg as soon as possible. Keep your weight low, on the footpegs, and use the controls and your upper body movements for balance and control.

Practice this technique separately and you'll see how

3. The brake-slide brings the bike into the main line. As soon as he gets off the brakes, Lamson is on the gas, as the slight roost tells us. His inside leg is out, ready to catch a slide. His torso leans forward, weighting the front wheel to plant it in the rut.

quickly it begins to work for you. Timing, balance, and anticipation give you control.

BRAKE OR ACCELERATE

When racing a motocross course, you should be either braking or accelerating, never coasting. Sometimes you're doing a little of each at the same time.

Now we're getting into the more advanced technical stuff that takes a lot of time and practice on the motorcycle. But this is what it takes to go fast and be in control.

Beginning riders are either braking, accelerating, or coasting. They usually do these things separately. They miss the benefit of controlling not only the motorcycle's speed and momentum but also the way it handles and holds the track.

A pro rider develops such fine feel and manipulation of the motorcycle that he can operate all the controls at the same time, with perfect control of each one. Many times, when a pro is going from braking to accelerating and from accelerating to braking, he's feathering the clutch and throttle and the front and rear brakes at the same time. This is at the transition point. And even when he isn't feathering them, he's going from one straight to the other. There is no coasting.

APPROACH DEX

The approach dex is where you go from accelerating to braking. There should be no coasting between.

You'll find an approach dex anytime you come upon an obstacle that causes you to make a transition from accelerating to braking. These can be found entering corners, before certain jumps, entering whoops, on downhills and drop-offs, and so on.

Beginning riders typically have a lot of room for improvement here. Beginners tend to go from accelerating to coasting, then braking, then usually more coasting, and braking again. The correct way is to go straight from accelerating to braking. Many times, accelerating and braking overlap. This makes the bike handle better and gives you more control over the situation.

Don't panic-brake; practice smooth, controlled braking.

EXIT DEX

The exit dex is where you go from braking to accelerating. Again, there should be no coasting between.

This is similar to the approach dex technique, but now we're talking about a different transition. The exit

4. On the exit, Lamson dials the throttle on. The front wheel is canted left a bit, indicating he's relying on a slight rear-wheel slide to bring the wheels in line and give him a straight drive out of the corner.

dex is most often found in corners. The common mistake is going from braking to coasting, then to accelerating. This makes the front wheel more likely to slide out.

In some corners, you should go from hard braking to hard accelerating, but more often you're going from hard braking (coming into the corner) to lighter and lighter braking, until you begin to lightly accelerate; after that, you accelerate hard. This means that the transition between braking and accelerating always has to be controlled, whether it's hard or light. Most of the time, braking and accelerating overlap.

There's a lot more to motocross than guts and glory. It's more like precision and control.

CONNECT THE DEXES

At the approach and exit dexes, you make smooth transitions from accelerating to braking and from braking to accelerating. You need to blend the forces of braking and accelerating just how and when you want with the controls. This requires mastery of all five controls.

Yes, we're still talking about the approach and exit dexes. This is because they're such important parts of motocross racing. One of the reasons is that there's a big transition between going from accelerating to braking and from braking to accelerating. Because of this big transition, it's necessary to do it correctly and have perfect control the whole time. If you control the front and rear brakes and the gearshift, clutch, and throttle properly, you'll have control. The proper use of these controls makes the motorcycle handle a certain way, depending on how you're using these controls.

For instance, when you're leaning the motorcycle over coming into a corner and you're dragging the rear brake, it pulls the front wheel back and to the inside. This keeps the front wheel from sliding out. As soon as you let go of the rear brake, you'd better be on the gas to maintain control, because if you coast, that's when the front wheel will slide out. That's only one example; there are several more. Just remember: accelerating or braking, never coasting.

FEATHER THE FRONT BRAKE

Feathering the front brake while going through a bermed corner will hold the front wheel in the berm and make the motorcycle turn more sharply.

The common mistake when entering bermed corners is to let go of the front brake too soon. The rider thinks he slowed down enough for the berm, so he

5. Again, Lamson is set up for a good drive. However, his wheels are not in line to drive out of the corner, because he's still pointed a bit wide. He needs to keep turning left, so he'll probably keep power application smooth and moderate by using the clutch and throttle. Once the bike is in the groove and pointed in the right direction, he opens up and drives hard to the next obstacle.

situation with this crude use of the controls. Also, some beginning riders use two, three, or even four fingers on the front brake. This is not good, because they can't hold onto the throttle as well. With disc brakes, one finger is all you need.

As we talked about earlier, you have to be able to control your speed and momentum at all times, especially at the approach and exit dexes. One of the ways to do this is to control both the front brake and throttle at the same time. Of course, you wouldn't use the front brake and throttle hard at the same time. By feathering the front brake and throttle at the same time, you have total control of your speed and momentum through the critical exit dex. This control also makes the motorcycle turn sharper and better.

If you're going to ride better, you're going to have to master these more precise techniques. The only way to do so is to practice.

FRONT BRAKE USE DURING BRAKE-SLIDES

When brake-sliding into a corner, use the front brake to target your pivot.

You can use the front brake as hard as you need to in this situation, because while the motorcycle is brake–sliding, the front wheel is tracking straight and will not slide out.

The front brake has more stopping power than the rear brake. Many riders lock up the rear brake in the corner to do a brake-slide, but they let go of the front brake way too early. When this happens, they have little control of where they pivot their brake-slide, because the motorcycle is just sliding in the turn. They have no stopping power.

When the motorcycle is brake-sliding, you can still use the front brake. The front wheel will be tracking straight and will not slide out. This way, you can come into the

releases the front brake. When the brake is released, the front wheel tends to go over the berm.

A pro keeps his finger on the front brake until he opens the throttle. Then he automatically lets go of the front brake. This means he has the ability to feather the front brake until he's ready to exit the berm hard.

When you're leaning over in a berm and you apply the front brake, it shortens the steering angle and slows the motorcycle, making it turn more sharply. The benefit is that you can come into a berm faster and still stay in it. This is especially true in right-hand corners, because you have to let go of the rear brake to put your foot out for the corner.

Learn to feather that front brake and throttle together through the exit dex (the transition between

braking and acceleration) in bermed corners and you'll never go over a berm again.

BRAKE/THROTTLE COORDINATION

You can feather the front brake and throttle at the same time. Use one finger on the front brake.

This is similar to the previous technique. Many techniques in motocross work together to give you overall control. In this case, we're talking about the control you'll have when you learn to feather the front brake and throttle together. This is done most often in bermed corners.

Many riders use only one control at a time. For example, they may let go of the front brake before they begin to use the throttle. You won't be in total control of the corner much faster and deeper and still pivot your brake-slide exactly where you want it.

Master using all the controls at the same time, not just one at a time.

BRAKE-SLIDE TO ACCELERATION

End your brake-slide where you want to turn and use the clutch, throttle, and brakes to go from brake-slide to power slide in one fluid motion.

When you want to square off a corner with a brake-slide and exit in a power slide, the brake-slide is the easy part. Heck, even little kids on their bicycles can do brake-slides. The tricky part is to pick up the power slide just before the brake-slide finishes off. If this isn't done correctly, the motorcycle will hesitate and do just about everything except what you want it to.

Make sure you brake-slide deep enough into the corner. When you're finished, you should be at least halfway around the corner. This way, you'll be facing the right way when you begin the power slide. Make sure your timing of letting go of the brakes and starting the power slide with the clutch and throttle is precise and controlled. You have to do it at the right time and with the right amount.

Practice making this transition on different surfaces, from tacky to slick.

BRAKE FOR CONTROL

Use the rear brake when entering a corner to hold the front wheel back and to the inside, keeping it from sliding out.

As we covered earlier, letting go of the front brake too early takes away your control. The same holds true with the rear brake. The common mistake a rider makes here is to let go of the rear brake when entering a corner. This eliminates your ability to slow down before the bike is facing the exit of the corner. This means you have to slow down early and give up control at the critical exit dex.

Your hardest braking should take place when you first shut the throttle off for the corner. This is where you need to scrub off the most speed quickly. Then, as you get further into the corner, you brake lighter and lighter all the way to the exit dex (where you go from braking to accelerating), where you finally let go of the brakes completely as you get on the clutch and throttle hard.

You'll feel the control when you learn to feather the rear brake to this point. No precision, no control.

Running in Too Deep

If you run it into a turn a little too deep, try not to panic. In this photo, Jimmy Button overshot the corner and concentrated on making the corner anyway. His rear wheel is over the berm, but his proper body positioning allows him to fix the problem easily.

Acceleration Bumps

1. This is a third-gear sweeper that's full of acceleration bumps. Team Honda's Ricky Carmichael has many choices here but chooses to apex early. This allows him to get on the gas early, to build speed for the 100-foot tabletop ahead.

2. By drifting wide, the multi-time AMA National Champion has a secondary benefit: he gets a better drive toward the acceleration bumps, which allows his suspension to work better.

3. Carmichael is a little crossed up, but that's okay. He's on the gas hard, and his front wheel is still pointing in the right direction. The rear wheel is searching for traction as it sprays topsoil, so it's stepped out a little bit, but RC is very much in control.

4. RC is almost at the exit point of the turn and is already upshifting. He keeps the front end light, which will help him skim across the tops of the bumps that occupy the exit of the turn.

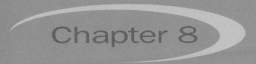

Chapter 8

JUMPS
The Search for Air

When learning to jump, experiment with different techniques. Try front- and rear-wheel landings at slow speeds, and try larger jumps only when you have a good idea how the bike will react to different jump faces, landing areas, terrain type, and dirt consistency. The world of motocross and off-road riding has hundreds of thousands of variables, and jumps are some of the most difficult obstacles to master. This is James Stewart using the bump-seat technique to get a little more lift than he would with the normal attack body position.

Few will argue that jumping a motorcycle is one of the most fun things in life. The sensation is incredible, and it's usually why riders choose off-road over street riding or road racing.

As you'll discover, all types of obstacles are used for grabbing air—everything from extremely slow-speed kickers to drop-offs to wide-open, top-speed jumps. Combine these with tabletop and combination jumps, such as doubles or triples, and you can see that there are many ways to initiate flight.

Jumps, however, require much respect, since they have the ability to punish you painfully for even minor mistakes. That's precisely why it's critical to ride within your limits at all times and resist the urge to become a daredevil.

The single most important thing to remember when learning to jump is to start with small obstacles. Make sure you're really comfortable jumping before you move on to larger obstacles. Learn on single jumps. Do not attempt tabletops, doubles, triples, or combination jumps until you've mastered single jumping.

Successful jumping depends on several factors, such as body position, timing, throttle and clutch control, bike setup, and realistic jump choice.

Look Before You Leap

Every jump should begin with careful analysis of the obstacle. Study the approach and look for any acceleration bumps, rocks, dirt

Being comfortable with jumping is important at all times. Travis Pastrana is one of the best jumpers in the world, and his style is proof that he's relaxed.

Jumping Fundamentals

1. Small jumps are good places to learn how a bike reacts. In this sequence, Danny Carlson demonstrates the fundamentals of jumping by standing with his knees bent, foot on the brake, arms up, elbows bent, eyes focused ahead.

2. As Carlson lifts off the ground, he uses his weight to balance the bike. He pushes out on the handlebar slightly, to keep the front end from rising, and weights the rear portion of the bike, so it doesn't kick him over the handlebar.

3. Carlson holds the position until he feels a correction needs to be made. If the front wheel were to rise, he might shift his weight forward. If it were to suddenly drop, he might pull up on the handlebar. If more drastic measures are required, he may hit the rear brake to drop the front—or gas it to spin, and drop, the rear wheel.

clods, ruts, or anything else that could interfere with you, your bike, and its suspension. Then study the face of the jump. Look for any lips that could kick you off balance or holes that could wreak havoc with your suspension. From there, inspect the landing area and look for a realistic location to land. Finally, before jumping, roll over the obstacle a few times to get your bearings.

"Before you jump, you should always be familiar with your surroundings," Jeremy McGrath says. "You should always know where you want to land—otherwise, you increase your chances of getting hurt."

After analyzing the jump and rolling over it a few times, you should have a fairly good understanding of how and at what angle it will toss you into flight. Your talent for making this determination will become much more clearly defined with experience.

Body Position

Most jumps require repositioning your body several times to maintain proper balance. That's why the generally preferred body position is to stand with your weight centered, knees and elbows bent, eyes focused ahead. This helps you make sudden movements on the bike and helps you soak up the impact of the jump more effectively.

Ideally, any movements on the bike to reposition your body should be done smoothly. Though speed is sometimes necessary, finesse is important—otherwise your own movements could upset the balance further.

Landing Attitude

On standard jumps, where you're landing on flat ground, the usual goal is to land both wheels at the same time. At higher speeds, however, most riders find it better to land with the front wheel approximately 6 inches higher than the rear. This reduces headshake upon impact, because the shock will hit first, reducing the likelihood of the front wheel wanting to wash out. Turning immediately after the jump usually warrants a front-wheel landing at slow (i.e., safe) speeds. With front-wheel landings, the front wheel should land about 6 inches lower than the rear wheel.

When landing front-wheel first, it's usually best to have your weight over the back of the seat and to stay off the front brake. This, along with a good stance that allows your knees and elbows to soak up the jolt, will reduce the chances of endoing.

4. As Carlson lands, he repositions his body toward the middle of the bike and soaks up the impact with his knees and elbows. Landing with the throttle on will ease the impact and get the bike driving as soon as possible.

5. Carlson holds the throttle on momentarily, to allow the engine to help maintain forward momentum—critical in helping the suspension absorb the energy. Had he wanted to brake immediately, the suspension would have undergone more strain and dipped further into the travel, perhaps even bottoming out.

Uphill and downhill landings usually warrant a flat style of landing, where both wheels come in contact with the ground at the same time. When there's a question of landing approach on single jumps, it's usually best to allow the rear wheel to touch down first.

Throughout all stages of the jump, the standing position permits the rider to control the attitude of the bike by pushing and pulling on the handlebar, allowing the bike to pivot somewhat on the footpeg axis while simultaneously moving rider weight frontward or backward. The photos illustrate this point.

"If you accidentally jump front-wheel low, you can sometimes get the bike to level out a little by pinning the throttle," Danny Carlson says. "The gyroscopic effect of the rear wheel has a lot of control over the bike. This is also why some riders tap the rear brake in the air to lower the front wheel. This also requires pulling in the clutch and giving the bike a few safety revs, so it doesn't stall in midair when the brake is activated."

"When I land, I usually try to match the angle of the bike with the ground, except in rough sections, where I'll keep the front wheel about half a foot high, so the fork doesn't

twist," states Ron Lechien. "If you land in a rough area with both wheels at the same time, you'll lose a lot of drive as the fork and shock rebound. If you land rear-wheel first with the throttle on, the shock won't spring back up so quickly, and you should get a better drive."

"Unless you're landing uphill or accidentally coming up short on a double jump, don't let the front wheel come up too high," says John Dowd. "The higher the front wheel gets, the harder it will slam down when you land."

It's also important to weight both footpegs equally, so you don't upset the bike's balance. Until you get into advanced jumping

Kicker Jumps

Watch out for kicker jumps, because their natural tendency is to kick riders over the handlebar. Kicker jumps are short, steep-faced jumps and bumps that toss the rear wheel substantially higher into the air than the front wheel. Approach the jump standing, at slow to moderate speed, with most of your body weight toward the rear of the seat. The faster you hit the jump, the more severe the kicking effect. Once you contact the jump, accelerate all the way off its face, to keep the front wheel high. On the face, try to provide resistance to the rear suspension by not allowing your knees to flex. If you attempt to soak up the jump with your knees, the effects of the shock rebounding will increase, and so will the likelihood of your going over the handlebars. However, don't lock your knees—you want to make sure you can move them if you need to reposition your weight at a moment's notice.

Changing Conditions

techniques, the idea is to keep the bike straight up and down and not leaned over to one side. A bike leaning over will have an increased chance of the wheels washing out on the jump face or the landing area, which could cause an assortment of unpleasant events. If this happens in the air, it may be corrected by adding weight to the footpeg that's higher, but this is a technique that should be used only when necessary.

Tabletops

Once you feel comfortable with single jumps, you may be ready to start jumping tabletops. This obstacle is like a double jump, but it's usually much safer, because the consequences of coming up short aren't as severe. Once again, the idea is to start small and work your way up to larger tabletop jumps.

After careful inspection and rolling the jump a few times, try to land on top of the tabletop, to get an idea how the jump will toss you and how much speed you'll need to clear the entire jump and land on the downslope. Continue landing on top, each time jumping a little farther (at a pace you feel comfortable with), until you start coming close to the end. You'll know when you're getting close, because your suspension will bounce you off the end of

the jump as it rebounds, and you won't have time to brake until you land at the very base of the jump.

In most cases, the idea is to jump front-wheel high (about 6 inches higher than the rear). This gives you greater control over the bike, in case you realize you've under- or over-jumped the obstacle. Ideally, if you matched your pace and think you'll land on the downslope, push forward on the handlebar, to begin lowering the front end of the bike. (As you push forward on the handlebar, your weight should move slightly forward, which will influence the bike's attitude.) Most riders prefer to have their bikes parallel to the ground at the midpoint of the jump and then slowly dip the front wheel during the later stages.

In most instances, you should match the bike angle to the landing ramp, which usually provides a soft landing. This is the same approach Alpine skiers use on the massive 100-meter-plus jumps, where they descend several stories. If a man jumped 50 feet straight down and landed on flat ground, odds are that the result would be tragic. When landing on a downslope, however, you decelerate at a slower pace and thus absorb the energy from the descent much better.

If you feel you're going to come up short and "case it," you usually want to hit the end

of the tabletop with both wheels at the same time, so you have more control over the bike. If you landed front-wheel first, you wouldn't be able to get a good drive (using the motor's power) to maintain control of the bike. If you overjump the tabletop, it's preferable to land in the same manner: flat, with the throttle on.

Fly Low

After you feel confident with tabletop jumps, you can try altering your technique. "On tabletop jumps, I always try to stay as low as possible," says Danny Carlson. "After I know I have enough momentum to clear the jump, I chop the throttle on the face of the jump, but only about the last two or three feet of it, and then push the handlebar forward once my front wheel lifts off the ground. I do this in one motion that causes my whole body to shift. The object is to redirect the bike, so it's going forward instead of upwards."

Doubles

If there ever comes a point in your life where you feel confident attempting double jumps, approach them in the same fashion as tabletop jumps. However, be forewarned that the penalty for underjumping them is often much more severe than for coming up short on a tabletop.

Ruts

Be careful on rut-filled approaches. Here, Tallon Vohland sits back on his bike, to allow his front end to settle into the rut as he drives off this high-speed double.

When possible, practice single jumping even to the point where you're almost landing at the base of the second jump (unless it's too big a leap—you be the judge). Single-jump practicing will once again be the best way to determine speed and get a good idea of trajectory. Only after you feel totally confident and ready should you attempt a double jump.

"Double jumping requires total commitment," says Steve Lamson. "You have to give it one hundred percent effort. Once you're in the air, there's no going back."

The angle of the bike on takeoff, in the air, and landing should be the same if you've calculated your distance correctly and will in fact land on the downside of the jump. When in doubt, it's better to overjump than underjump, because the penalties are generally less painful. It all depends on the landing area and how much room you have before the next obstacle.

While overjumping doubles requires the same technique as overjumping tabletops, underjumping is much different. It's usually best to land front-wheel high if you're coming up way short and plan to land on the face of the jump. The impact will be severe, and this method allows both the fork and the shock to take the hit simultaneously. If you're going to case it—land with one wheel on either side of the jump—you should do so with the bike parallel to the ground. If you case it with the front wheel lower than the rear, there's a good chance you'll endo. If you case it front-wheel high, the rear suspension will rebound wildly and could cause you to do a number of strange things, none of them good.

"When you're learning how to double jump, start out small and then work your way up," says Danny Carlson. "It's also a good idea to find jumps to practice on where the second one is rounded, so the consequences won't be so bad if you come up short."

Triple Jumps

Triples require the same approach as doubles—work up to them. Begin by rolling the jumps, then landing between the first two, then double, then overjump the double (if possible), until you feel like tripling. Once you triple, pretend the middle jump doesn't exist and treat it as a long double.

Double Jumps

1. Double jumps are a frequently used component of modern-day tracks. The idea is to jump over the second obstacle and land on its backside. For illustration, we're using a 70-foot triple jump to show the ways to double and triple. It all starts with the approach and getting a good drive toward the jump face. In this photo, Danny Carlson is standing with his weight centered. His knees are bent to absorb some of the impact, and his elbows are bent so his body can flow as the bike starts to go vertical. He's already determined he has enough speed to double the jump, but he has to be cautious that he doesn't overjump the obstacle and land on the face of the third jump—or on flat land, for that matter.

2. As Carlson hits the face of the jump, he's still standing straight, but look at the gap between the handlebar and his stomach in this photo and the previous one. The bars have come into his chest as the front wheel starts to come up, but he's still in a neutral body position.

3. In the previous photo, Carlson had his weight centered, but notice how he shifts his body to the back of the bike. This is the result of pushing on the handlebar to lower the front end. When the landing area is on a downward slope, it's preferable to match the attitude of the bike with the landing zone.

4. As both wheels lift off, Danny adjusts his body position to control the attitude of the bike. He shifts his body forward, which helps keep the front end from coming up too high. This is a critical step in the jump process. If your weight is too far back, you can loop out. If it's too far forward, you can endo. Double jumps are dangerous in general, so it's best to start off small and slowly build up to larger jumps when you've determined you have the skills.

5. This is a pulled-back view of the entire triple jump. Carlson has successfully managed to lower the front wheel. It's only a foot higher than the rear wheel, which gives him good overall control. If it looks like he needs to make adjustments to the height of the front wheel, he can shift his weight forward to lower it or lean back to raise it. His body position will move it only slightly, but it can help during landing. Most of the bike's attitude is controlled during takeoff. Midair adjustments can help, but the techniques, such as the rear brake tap, are usually reserved for advanced riders.

6. Midway over the gap, Carlson's Suzuki is nearly parallel to the ground. At this point, he's transitioning his weight and preparing for the landing.

7. As Carlson starts his descent, he begins lowering the front end of the bike once he realizes he's going to land on the downside of the second jump. If he were accidentally coming up short, he'd want to keep the front wheel high, but he's calculated his distance perfectly.

8. Danny has shifted his weight to the back of the bike once again. This will help him absorb the impact from the 350-plus pounds coming into contact with the ground.

9. Still standing, Carlson can absorb the impact with his knees and elbows. His suspension does a good job of sucking up the harsh landing.

Triples

This is the same jump we used to illustrate the double jump. Big-air triple jumps like this are impressive and challenging. Because of the altitude and speeds involved, they're also some of the riskiest jumps, requiring huge amounts of skill, confidence, and commitment. In most cases, it's best to work your way up to triple jumps by first singling each jump until you feel comfortable double-jumping. Only after you have confidence double-jumping and feel you can successfully tackle the entire obstacle should you think about tripling.

Before any double, triple, or tabletop jump, the approach is always pivotal to success. To clear the jump, you have to have enough acceleration, which usually requires a straight,

bump-free run at the takeoff jump. On the jump face, the suspension will absorb some of the impact, which can be seen as Danny Carlson nearly bottoms the rear end. On takeoff, it's important to have the engine in the powerband, keep your body weight centered, and stand up, so you can use your knees to soak up some of the shock.

To get the best drive, Carlson accelerates all the way off the face of the jump, which causes the front end to rise faster than the rear. To balance out this effect, he pushes away on the handlebar slightly, which also shifts his weight to the back of the seat. This allows the bike to pivot on the footpeg axis. In the air, it's best to stay a little loose, so you can adjust the attitude of the bike if needed. In most cases use finesse instead of muscle to control the flight pattern.

As Carlson prepares to land, he begins to readjust the attitude of the bike to match the downslope of the landing area. Once again he pushes down on the handlebar, causing his weight to slide back even further. As the front end drops rapidly, his butt begins to touch the rear portion of the seat. Though it appears he's sitting, he's actually still standing.

A split second before touching down, Carlson returns his body to the centered position, standing with his knees and elbows bent, to absorb the impact. This particular uphill triple jump is followed by a corner, so he has to brake instead of accelerating.

1. Drop-off jumps can be tricky, because the result is usually a harsh impact. The idea is to go off the jump with your weight toward the back of the bike—standing, but crouched. As the bike drops, extend your legs to maintain control. It's usually also wise to jump front-wheel high, because it provides more control on landing.

2. You can see how John Dowd extends his knees to handle the effects of the sudden drop. His front wheel is approximately 6 inches higher than the rear, and his body is close to the attack position.

3. The harsh landing is softened as Dowd collapses his knees and elbows. As the roost indicates, he's hard on the throttle, which also softens the blow through the use of increased forward momentum. This forward momentum technique is the same one that allows Alpine ski jumpers to soar over 100 meters and drop several stories without any suspension.

4. Immediately after landing, Dowd continues to accelerate to the next obstacle in the standing attack position.

Elevated Doubles

Another type of double or triple incorporates an uphill, where the intent is to ascend to a different elevation. In this instance, you continue working up to the jump at your own pace, but once you decide to commit, the idea is usually to match the angle of the landing area—which in most cases will be flat.

Matching the angle is the same idea used for downhill double or triple jumps. However, the penalty for jumping short is intensified, since it's much more difficult to lose momentum when traveling downhill. If you clip the final jump with either wheel, it's extremely difficult to control the bike's angle.

Drop-Offs

One of the final types of jumps is the drop-off. Typically, try to land with the front wheel 6 to 12 inches off the ground, which allows the suspension to work its best. In most instances, the landing area of drop-offs will be filled with chuckholes caused by erratic acceleration of bikes landing all over the place. The acceleration will help your suspension absorb the impact.

"Front-wheel landings are usually only a good idea when landing on smooth ground that won't mess with your suspension," says Lamson. "Most of the time, front-wheel landings are only used when you have to get on the brakes quickly after a jump or on the downside of a double, triple, or tabletop jump where a corner or another obstacle immediately follows."

If you're jumping in an area that's difficult to judge, Mike Healey has a suggestion: "On blind jumps, where I can't see the landing area on the approach, I always try to find reference points, so I make sure I land in the right area. Most of the time I'll follow the line that's been worked into the ground, but sometimes I have to use trees, rocks, or other land markings for reference."

Sitting Down on the Job

While standing is the most widely used body position for jumping, sitting may be preferable at times. Sitting on takeoff provides additional lift but should be done only if conditions are perfect. It requires a smooth, bump-free approach to the jump and a gradual jump face. Sitting usually allows the bike to get tossed higher and farther off the jump, because it doesn't allow your knees to soak up any of the shock on takeoff. Therefore, the suspension is compressed farther on the jump face and then generally rebounds more quickly on takeoff. The quicker rebound is one of the key factors that ultimately determines height and distance.

Regardless of the type of jump, be familiar with your engine's power characteristics, so your bike doesn't do anything unexpected. If you're tackling an uphill double or triple jump and your bike can't produce enough drive, it's important to know that beforehand.

"Keep a finger on the clutch in case the bike bogs at any time, especially when you land," Lechien recommends. "If you're landing on an uphill or if you naturally lose a lot of momentum in the air, you may have to downshift before you land, so you can continue your drive."

Ultimately, good jumping depends on rider skill and how well you can read the terrain and alter your technique appropriately.

JUMPS

- **Start with small jumps at slow speeds.**
- **In most instances, maintain a neutral body position on the bike.**
- **Typically, the idea is to stand on takeoff, in midair, and while landing.**
- **Adjust your body positioning in the air to control the bike's attitude.**
- **Use your knees and elbows to help the suspension absorb the impact.**
- **Use the motor's acceleration to help the suspension soak up energy while landing.**
- **Landing on downslopes is typically much easier on the suspension and the rider.**
- **Whenever possible, avoid landing with the brakes on.**
- **If you're in the air for an extended period, rev the engine as much as necessary to keep it from stalling.**
- **When jumping double, triple, or tabletop jumps, the usual goal is to land on the downslope and avoid clipping the top portion of the landing area.**

Gary Semics on Jumps

"Courage is resistance to fear, mastery of fear, not absence of fear."

— Mark Twain

The emphasis on jumping in motocross cannot be overstated. Supercross is all about jumping and timing, and motocross tracks have changed to incorporate supercross-style obstacles. To win today, you must master the air as well as the earth.

The key to controlling the jump is at takeoff. By using the correct technique and practicing until jumping is natural and relaxed, you can have complete control over your airborne machine.

Combination Jumps

Some tracks feature combination jumps like this. Though combination jumps come in all shapes, sizes, and styles, this one consists of a small jump onto a cluster of tabletop jumps, followed by another single jump. There are many ways to tackle this, and we're going to show you Danny Carlson's method for taking them with as few leaps as possible. This combines several jumping techniques, and all combo jumps are different—it's the nature of the beast.

In jumps such as this, confidence and timing are everything. Had Carlson not landed in the right place, he might have gotten a bad suspension bounce and/or lost his drive to clear the small double jump at the end, but he executed this entire jump perfectly.

His front wheel is higher than the rear during the first half of flight. If he came up short, he'd maintain the stance, to help the suspension soak up the impact more efficiently. However, he did, in fact, have enough momentum to readjust his body position and eventually match his angle with the downslope of the final jump.

JUMP HIGHER

To jump higher and farther, load the suspension just before take-off and help it unload on takeoff.

Be careful when practicing this technique. Start off small and work your way up gradually, as you gain confidence and control.

The most common mistake is for the rider to tense up or freeze in the critical part of the jump, which occurs upon compression and rebound as the motorcycle leaves the ground. By freezing, the rider is left at the mercy of inertia.

The correct way to jump is to use your body weight to help the suspension compress just before it starts to rebound. Then you want to help the suspension rebound, by lifting your weight out of the suspension just as it begins to rebound. At the same time, adjust the angle of your upper body to control the height of the front wheel as the motorcycle is in the air.

The most important part of the jump is where the motorcycle leaves the ground. What's going to happen at this point? You guessed it—compression and rebound. Rather than tensing up, key into it and go with the flow.

JUMP LOWER

Absorb the compression and rebound part of the jump with your body when you want less height and distance on a jump. Let the motorcycle come up under you by giving a little in your elbows and knees.

Most beginning riders don't know the difference between jumping far and high or jumping shorter and lower to get back on the ground quickly and gain time. They just jump with the same technique and style every time. There's definitely a big difference in these two techniques.

Simply put, jumping the motorcycle shorter and lower is pretty much the opposite of jumping higher. In this situation, you want to help the motorcycle absorb the compression and rebound part of the jump with your body movements. You want to suck the bike up under you when you jump. This way, you can cover the jumps faster and get back on the ground smoother and quicker.

Practice both ways and you'll notice a big difference. Of course, practice on a safe jump.

AERIAL ADJUSTMENTS

While the motorcycle is airborne, pulling in the clutch and locking up the rear wheel will make the front wheel drop slightly. Grabbing a handful of throttle will make the front wheel rise slightly.

Although the most important part of the jump is where the motorcycle leaves the ground, you still have to control it through the air to set up for your landing. As with the launch, you need to be relaxed and loose in the air. Don't be a panic jumper.

Once the bike is in the air, you can control it to a degree with your body. In addition, the clutch and throttle can give you some interesting gyroscopic effects.

You can drop the front end slightly, by pulling the clutch in and hitting the rear brake to lock up the rear wheel. Suddenly stopping the spinning force of the rear wheel will cause the front end to drop. The faster the rear wheel is spinning, the more the front will drop.

Grabbing a handful of throttle and suddenly spinning the rear wheel faster will cause the front wheel to rise. This is called panic revving, because you've got your front wheel too low and you don't care how much noise you're making as long as you save it.

It's not a good idea to lock up the front wheel while airborne. Oh yeah, it'll drop the front end, but it can cause a squirrelly landing because the front wheel will still be stopped when you land.

So you see, the controls of the motorcycle are important even when the wheels are in the air.

TURNING IN THE AIR

When you want to turn the motorcycle in the air, lean, turn, and whip the rear end over as you take off the jump. While you're in the air, maintain the center of balance and straighten it out before you land.

You may have seen some beginning riders trying to whip it sideways through the air, and all that ends up happening is that they turn the front wheel.

When you want to throw it sideways, you have to set up as you approach the jump. The most important part happens as the motorcycle leaves the jump. You have to lean, turn, and whip it as you take off. Then you have to maintain the center of balance with your body positions and movements while you make adjustments through the air. If you're having trouble straightening it upon landing, it's most likely because you're not maintaining the center of balance with your body movements.

You pretty much have to commit yourself to how much you're going to get leaned over and sideways as you leave the jump. This technique can be fairly dangerous, so be very careful. Practice step by step on a good safe takeoff and landing. A big step-up jump is the safest.

Although this technique is mostly for show, it does have other benefits. You can set up for a corner in the air and can be turning as you land. Also, this technique can prepare for the inevitable time when you come off a jump out of shape.

Nowadays, just riding on the ground is not enough. You have to be able to fly, too.

This rider comes up short and lands on top of the third jump of this triple. Fortunately, he's using the proper technique and absorbs most of the impact with his knees and elbows, which act as additional suspension.

Rear-wheel landings are not preferable on big jumps, because they make the fork feel harsher than flat landings on the downslope. This is called a "slap down" and usually happens when riders adjust their body when they feel they'll come up short. If you do come up short, this may be one of the only techniques that can save you from disaster. Then again, it's never pleasant to come up short.

1. This rider comes up way short on the same triple jump. Had he landed flat or with his front wheel first, he probably would have endoed. As is, he's still going to experience a wild ride.

2. Upon initial impact, the suspension bottoms hard and rebounds the rider fast. This sends his bike and body into an endo, and all he can do is reposition his body to the back of the bike and hang on.

3. As the endo gets worse, it's important to stay off the front brake.

4. This is one of the critical points in this attempt to avoid crashing. The rider needs to keep his weight on the back of the bike but is having a difficult time.

5. The rider begins to lose his battle. His arms start to buckle, and his body starts to move forward on the bike. Because of this he eventually endoed, but the rest of the sequence occurred out of camera range.

Chapter 9

RUTS
Mind Over Matter

Ruts can be intimidating, but they can be conquered with proper knowledge, confidence, and good technique.

Ruts are unlike any other obstacle. Deep channels typically give you the least amount of control over your motorcycle while still leaving you "in control." Once both tires drop into a narrow groove, you're more or less along just for the ride and can do little to change direction. In fact, you can do more harm than good. If you, you'll probably end up out of shape or on the ground. If you relax and ride with the rut, you'll be just fine.

Though ruts are usually unpleasant and cause a lot of riders grief, there are some strategies to make them much easier and more user-friendly.

"Always scan ahead to see where the rut leads and if it branches out into other lines," says Guy Cooper. "If you aren't paying attention, you could wind up getting stuck or led way out of your way."

"Monitor the ruts around the entire track, to see how rapidly they're getting deeper," instructs John Dowd. "You'll be surprised at how fast good lines can deteriorate. Therefore, you've got to keep a sharp eye out for better lines."

Careful rut analysis is the first step toward successful completion. In many cases, alternative rut-free lines will be available that would normally be considered out of the way. But when you do have to ride ruts, there are other things to remember.

"The goal with any rut is to enter the line as straight as possible, so you can flow with the line," says Guy Cooper. "You want to make sure both wheels can smoothly get into the groove, thus helping you maintain the most control over your bike. If you get the front wheel in but the back end is still out, or vice versa, then you'll be cross-rutted. When you're cross-rutted, you aren't able to maintain total control, which will cripple your speed and possibly cause you to crash.

"I've found that there isn't a single universal riding style that works well for riding ruts all the time," adds Cooper. "However, I've found that keeping the front end light in straightaways and not fighting the bike seems to work the best. In turns, I've learned that a less aggressive approach works well, but the real trick is line selection."

"In ruts that are really deep, you have to be careful that your lower fork tubes don't get caught," instructs Steve Lamson. "The same thing can happen with your footpegs, swingarm, and chain guide. If any one of these scrapes too much, it will rob you of momentum and possibly cause you to crash. In deep ruts, try to keep your toes pointed upwards, so they don't snag on the rut walls. If your foot catches, it will instantly rip your

Good rut-riding skills can make the difference between finishing and having to push your bike off the track. Ruts can also be turned to your advantage, either for passing or to hold a clean line.

foot off the bike, and there's nothing you can do about it."

Typically, you have to go slower in ruts than normal, because you'll have a more difficult time maintaining your balance.

"Try to stay fluid on the bike," recommends Ron Lechien. "Any abrupt movements could cause you to lose your balance. This is definitely one place where finesse pays off."

"Before you enter a rut, it's usually a good idea to make sure you've finished all your braking," says Mike Healey. "I'm not saying you can't brake while you're in a rut—you have to do it every once in a while. I'm just saying you'll have less control, and the front end is more likely to twist."

Plan Your Attack

1. When approaching a series of ruts, analyze the situation carefully. Choose the shallowest groove that provides the straightest shot to the next obstacle. In this sequence, Mike Craig is using finesse to get a smooth launch off the jump.

2. Instead of turning the bike to correct a balance problem, Craig simply shifts his body to the right. While in the rut, let the bike ride in it naturally (rather than climbing out of the rut) and concentrate on the obstacle ahead. Work the wheel slightly left and right, adjusting to keep the front wheel in the center of the rut.

1. A jump leads into this tight left-hand turn and requires a variety of techniques used together. Chad Reed jumps short, so he can brake in time to set up for the tight rutted turn that follows.

2. Reed spots his line and tries to finish braking as his suspension collapses. The braking effect will cause the front end of the suspension travel to drop deeper into the stroke, making the landing harsher than normal.

3. The factory Yamaha rider transitions to the seated position as the front end deflects off a braking bump.

4. He still works both brakes and starts to lower his inside foot for balance as he enters the turn.

5. The Australian uses a small amount of front brake to keep his front wheel from riding over the entrance of the rut. This braking technique allows him to carry more momentum into the turn while staying in control.

6. He leans into the turn and hasn't gotten on the gas yet. You can barely tell, but he's still on the brakes until he reaches the apex of the turn.

7. The factory Yamaha rider gets on the gas once he feels he won't overshoot the turn. He uses the power to pull the bike through the turn but keeps his weight forward, so the front wheel has traction. If the front wheel loses traction, the front end of the bike will wander.

8. Reed accelerates hard out of the turn and at this point has pretty much finished the difficult part. Now he needs to think about the next obstacles that lie ahead and whether he needs to be sitting or standing in the next few feet.

Rutted Corners

1. In this sequence James Dobb enters the rutted turn perfectly and at the proper speed. All of his braking was done well in advance. Notice that his elbows are up, his inside foot is out for balance, his eyes are focused ahead, and he appears to be in total control. What you can't see is that Dobb is weighting his outside footpeg, which helps the bike stay balanced.

2. Dobb continues to make a gradual arch and hasn't changed his body position. At this point he's rolling on the throttle slowly in order to rocket out of the turn. A word of caution: too much throttle or clutch action could cause the front wheel to jump out of the line and spoil the perfect turn.

3. Dobb is accelerating hard, as evidenced by the slight wheelie. Notice that the bike is actually oversteering as his suspension rebounds upon the exit. Dobb has shifted his weight forward in an aggressive manner.

4. Dobb has successfully executed the turn and is focused on the next obstacle. Notice how his head is directly over the handlebar to keep the bike from wheelying. This rut was very tacky and traction was abundant.

Avoiding Ruts

In the same turn where James Dobb railed the line perfectly, Larry Ward has chosen a more aggressive approach. Ward has gone up on the banking, which is full of traction, and has opted to square off the turn and avoid the rut altogether. Ward crosses perpendicular to the rut so the groove doesn't catch his front wheel. In essence, he's treating the rut like a small hole and simply allowing his suspension to absorb it as he accelerates to the next obstacle.

Deep Ruts

1. This is a classic example of a rutted corner. As you can see, there are lines all over the place. Even in this moderately deep rut, Steve Lamson is already scraping the chain guide against the inside rut wall, which makes cornering much more challenging.

2. Lamson gets on the gas harder as he approaches the exit of the corner and the front end starts to lift. Had he been mid-rut, his small wheelie might have forced his front wheel over the rut wall, which can easily cause a rider to crash.

Even 9-inch ruts down a straightaway can be tricky. The key is to keep your weight on the back of the bike and keep the front end light. This way, the bike will guide itself through the turn as much as possible, self-correcting along the journey. Don't be fooled—ruts like these are never easy.

RUTS

Mike Healey—"Most of the time, ruts are the result of too much moisture, like rain or overwatering a track with a water truck. If it does rain, use hand guards to keep your hands and grips dry."

Danny Carlson—"Watch for rocks that may be sticking out of the groove, because they can cause you to throw a chain. If this worries you, make sure your chain, sprockets, and chain guides are all in good condition and tightened to spec."

Ken Faught—"It's very important to enter the rut straight, so you get both wheels into the groove. If you enter a rutted corner too fast, you run the risk of jumping out of the rut and cross-rutting. This is when your wheels are outside the line, which will ultimately slow your drive."

Mike Healey—"If the ruts are extremely deep and there's no way around them, consider raising your shift lever one position and repositioning the rear brake pedal. It will feel awkward when you ride, but at least they won't snag as much."

Railing Ruts

When used effectively, ruts can actually be the hot ticket around a turn because they provide resistance, which serves the same purpose as bankings in automotive racing. Here, Mike LaRocco rails the turn with surgical perfection and gets so much traction that he is able to wheelie while leaning way over.

Shane Watts—"I usually sit down in rutted corners, to lower my center of gravity and enable myself to dab a foot if needed. In straight ruts I usually stand, so I can be light on the bike and allow the front wheel to bounce off rut walls with less resistance."

Dick Burleson—"I usually look for the shortest rut with the least amount of turns. There are some ruts that can be a big advantage, and there are cases when they can be like minefields. Like everything, the difference between the good, the bad, and the ugly is situational. One important thing to remember is, look for the endpoint of any rut before you ride into it. Make sure it's not going to lead you off course."

Descending Ruts

Riding in a descending rut can be extremely tricky, especially one that comprises the exit of a turn. Typically, the front wheel wants to jump out of the line under acceleration. But too much weight on the front end could cause the rear wheel to lift out of its groove. Patience, liberal throttle application, and centered seat positioning are all qualities that work well in this situation, as James Dobb demonstrates.

Climbing a Rut Wall

Mike LaRocco's wheel has started to ride the outside of the rut wall and now wants to jump out of its line. To settle the front end, LaRocco backed off the throttle and leaned further into the inside of the corner, which allowed the bike to make corrections.

Chapter 10

WHOOPS
Timing and Rhythm Are Key

Whoops are some of the most challenging obstacles, period. They're designed that way. In a nutshell, whoops are usually created to break up a rider's momentum, to test skill, endurance, line selection, and motorcycle setup.

Because of the many types of whoops, few guidelines can be used with any frequency. Some whoops require a double- or triple-jump technique to be used repeatedly, while others mandate a skimming approach for quicker navigation.

Body Position

The most important thing that will make you a better whoop rider is body position. In nearly every instance, the idea is to stand all the way through the whoop section. This allows you to absorb some of the shock with your

Try as many lines as possible in practice, and be prepared to adjust your lines during the race. Whoops typically change as the race progresses, and the fast line may move around. Whoops can be a good place to pass, as long as you take a different line than the rider in front of you. That way, you'll be poised to take advantage of any mistakes.

The attack position is the preferred riding position and the basis for most whoop riding. Ernesto Fonseca shifts his weight back, to keep the bike level. In most cases, the front wheel should be level with or above the rear wheel through the whoops.

Keeping It Straight

Effective whoop riding technique requires the straightest shot possible at each successive whoop. This is the only way the suspension will be able to do its job effectively—otherwise, the rear end will wander, which could lead to major swapping.

Doubling Whoops

Because this row of whoops has a major gap at the beginning, John Dowd alters his style accordingly and prefers to double-jump into the section. He uses an advanced sit-down approach. This gives him more lift, because the shock rebounds more quickly than in the normal standing position. The maneuver is difficult, because it also kicks the rear end up rapidly and causes the front wheel to drop suddenly.

arms and legs. You'll need to shift your body position as you go through whoops, but your body should be a bit back of center most of the time. In deep, wide-spaced whoops, skim the front tire from peak to peak. In this case, your body position will shift back a bit (but not so far that you're hanging out over the rear fender). When the whoops are more abrupt and tightly spaced, stay centered and let the front and rear of the bike soak up the impacts. The key here is to stay centered and let the bike rock back and forth when it hits a bump.

Heads Up!

Stay alert and keep at least a finger or two on the clutch and front brake, in case you have to stop quickly. Pay attention at all times, because whoop sections are unpredictable. Never get too confident, or they may bite you.

Front Wheel High

Most success in navigating whoops is determined by the initial approach. Most, but not all, require riders to enter the whoop section with the front wheel high. Keep the front end light, so it can skim over the top of shallow whoop sections. When using this skimming technique, keep your weight toward the back of the bike. Too much weight on the front wheel could cause the bike to stab a whoop and send you over the handlebar.

Work your way up to speed on every type of whoop you encounter. Riding too aggressively could land you on your head.

Steve Lamson finds the fast line through a set of whoops. Although his weight is back, he's trying to keep the bike as level as possible.

The only time your front wheel should be this high is if you're starting from a near dead stop. This way, you can wheelie over a whoop or two to begin a good drive.

Doubling and Tripling

Aside from skimming-type whoops, you'll most likely encounter whoops that are too far apart to skim but close enough to double-, triple-, or even quadruple-jump. If that's the case, resort to regular jumping techniques.

"On whoops that you're jumping instead of skimming, try not to overjump them when you're doubling," recommends Steve Lamson. "If you land on the face of another jump, your suspension may rebound you kind of weird, and it may not toss you where you want to go. Your suspension will also get screwed up if you come up short or case it. The best way is usually the smoothest."

"If you're jumping the whoops, use your legs to get a little extra lift," Ron Lechien adds. "Before the first whoop, bend your knees to the point where you're almost sitting, then push down really hard on the face of the jump, which will further compress the suspension. As you push down, your legs will straighten up momentarily, and then you'll need to bend them quickly (once again) as the bike lifts off the ground. All this has to happen in a split second to work."

"Keep an eye on the whoops throughout your race," Mike Craig adds. "Sometimes a better line will develop as the race progresses."

Gary Semics on Whoops

"Every failure brings with it the seed of an equivalent success."

— Napoleon Hill

Mastering whoops requires good body position and great timing. Most jumping techniques also apply to whoops.

Skimming Whoops

1. This is a prime example of a man-made whoop section. The whoops are fairly close to one another and are about a foot and a half tall. Danny Carlson enters the whoop section standing, with his weight centered, knees and elbows bent, but adds a little weight to the front end as he crests the top of the lead whoop. The added weight on the front end will help set him up so he can get the bike parallel to the ground, which is necessary to get the best drive in this skimming-type whoop section.

ROW THE BOAT

Time the rowing action of your body with the compression and rebound of bumps and other obstacles on the track. You need to row back as the rear wheel tries to kick up.

Many riders just ride the motorcycle across rough ground or whoops and never try to time how they weight and unweight the suspension. The result is that the motorcycle ends up weighting and unweighting their bodies with a mind of its own.

This technique requires good timing and anticipation. You have to anticipate where you're going to weight and unweight the motorcycle (to help the suspension compress and rebound) to make it skip, jump, fly, and land just how and where you want it to. This is not just a straight-up-and-down movement. While you're helping the suspension compress and rebound, you have to move back and forth to keep the motorcycle somewhat level.

Learn to do this right, because I guarantee you, it feels good and you'll live longer.

2. Carlson quickly adjusts the attitude of the bike so it's parallel to the ground. The idea is to skim across the tops of the whoops (not allowing either wheel to dip into the trough). This photo perfectly illustrates how Carlson strives to make contact with each whoop to maintain maximum drive.

THROTTLE LAUNCH

Use the clutch and throttle to launch you out of whoops, jumps, and certain kinds of bumps.

As we mentioned before, a common mistake is to use just the throttle instead of the clutch and throttle together. To launch the bike with the throttle, you need precise timing of the power hit to the rear wheel. If you use just the throttle, you're not always going to be able to match the right amount of power and timing to the rear wheel.

In this case, the clutch is used more like a trigger. You want to trigger the clutch with the correct timing of the throttle as the bike compresses into the jump or whoop. This technique gives you better control of your launch and more height and distance.

Practice this carefully on larger, sharp-edged bumps, small tabletops, or other safe jumps before trying it on big jumps.

3. Occasionally, even the best riders in the world have to let one wheel or the other dip into a trough. When this happens, the idea is to rebuild momentum quickly, which usually requires double-jumping the next whoop, landing on the downslope, and then readjusting body position to get the bike parallel to the ground.

4. Effective whoop riding always combines careful throttle control and clutch use with continual repositioning of your body. Although whoops are small, be careful. These are some of the trickiest obstacles on any track. Even the end of a whoop section can be tricky, so don't lose concentration until you're in the clear.

5. Avoid dropping the front wheel into the face of a whoop at high speeds. This is a recipe for disaster, even if you're talented and strong, like Danny Carlson. Fortunately, he recovers by shifting his weight to the back of the bike and extending his arms, so they can act like shock absorbers upon impact.

Chapter 11

OFF-ROAD OBSTACLES
Nature's Way of Fighting Back

Obstacles encompass some of the greatest joys (and pains) of off-road riding. In motocross or even some hare scrambles and cross-country races, you see obstacles several times and work up to crossing at speed. Enduro and trail riders, on the other hand, typically encounter these gifts from Mother Nature unexpectedly and only a few times. Riders have to think quickly and learn to adapt their techniques to rapidly changing conditions and obstacles that loom around every corner. For this reason, off-road riding is a great way to improve your skills. It forces you to be creative and deal with situations quickly and efficiently.

For each of these obstacles—trees, rocks, water crossings, and so on—certain techniques will help you get over them speedily and in one piece.

Trees

Trees are some of the least forgiving obstacles on the planet. In essence, they're like tall, skinny rocks with arms and are capable of causing great pain with a single, glancing blow.

Because trees can grow almost anywhere, their presence can make even the simplest obstacles far more treacherous. Hence, the rule of thumb is to avoid trees! Like an Aikido master, they approach violence passively: if you don't hit them, they won't hurt you.

Sometimes the best way to go fast through trees is to go slow. You'll lose some time, but going slow is better than going fast

Many riders, such as Ty Davis, cut their handlebars down so they can squeeze through trees much more easily. As you can see, many trails offer little room to negotiate. This photo also illustrates why it's important to keep your elbows tucked in.

for a little while, crashing, and going fast some more until you crash again. Mistakes can be extremely time-consuming, and they waste lots of energy.

"Near trees, I ride with my knees tucked in as close to the bike as possible, to prevent my legs from getting hit," says Guy Cooper. "I also try to keep my toes pointed in, so they don't snag on anything.

"Pay close attention to width when you're splitting two trees," adds Cooper. "If you're not sure if you can safely make it through, then you should stop. If it's too narrow to attack at speed, usually you can push one end of the handlebar through at a time, kind of wiggling your way on by, and then continue."

On the same note, Scott Summers adds, "If you ever have to ride under a fallen tree,

The shortest distance between two points is a straight line. When trees obscure the path, riders frequently try to get as close as possible to them, only to discover the painful penalty of getting too close. *Ken Faught*

Woods riders use sturdy aluminum or plastic hand guards to prevent hand injuries. Even low-speed collisions can break fingers, hands, wrists, arms, elbows, and other bones. Good hand guards, such as these from Moose Racing, also prevent the levers from being bent or broken. *Ken Faught*

TREES

- Watch out for roots that can be hidden under leaves.
- Keep an eye out for low branches that could knock you off your bike.
- When splitting two trees, make sure you have enough room to safely negotiate.
- When riding under a fallen tree, make sure you have enough room to squeeze by, and remember that a helmet and drink system add height when you're in a crouched position.

"Watch out for tree branches that could knock you off your bike or jab you like a spear," says Cooper. "These can be as dangerous as the trees themselves, and they can easily be disguised."

Because branches are usually found in shaded areas with limited visibility, pay close attention to your surroundings at all times.

And wherever you find trees, you're bound to find tree roots. Remember, the closer you are to a tree, the larger the root. Unfortunately, roots can also easily be camouflaged by a lack of sunlight and surrounding foliage. Small bushes and leaves can give riders a false sense of security, but it takes only one encounter with roots to remember their painful potential.

Rocks

It's hard to imagine, but a 100-yard-long rock bed can be as damaging to both man and machine as a 100-mile section of normal trail. Rocks are harder than terra firma and therefore become more damaging, even when a crash occurs at low speed. Simply put, most suspensions don't know how to react when they contact something that doesn't want to give, even a little bit.

make sure you have plenty of headroom. If there's any question in your mind, come to a complete stop for further inspection and then proceed. There may be broken branches or other things that could cause you injury."

It's fairly common for riders to underestimate their overall height when riding under trees. It's easy to forget that a helmet adds almost 2 inches, and some people fail to realize that even if they're ducking, with their chin resting on the gas tank or seat, and they hit a tree, their head can't go down any further. The result could injure the rider's head, neck, back, or all three.

Riders also tend to forget that their drink system, if used, adds a couple of inches to their height when they're crouched over. It's not uncommon to see riders get momentarily stuck because their drink system has caused them to get wedged between their bike and a fallen tree.

Also watch out for downed trees lying on the ground (see the upcoming section on log crossings). Nothing will send you over the handlebar quicker than hitting an immovable object.

Aside from tree trunks, you have to avoid several other items.

TREES

Guy Cooper—"I always cut my bars when I know that I'll encounter trees. Usually, they are less than 30 inches wide. However, this is one area where it's best to experiment to come up with your own width."

Scott Summers—"I wear forearm and elbow guards to protect myself from any contact."

Shane Watts—"Try to look for the straightest path possible in the trees, and watch out for tree roots. Usually there are a lot of leaves covering the ground, and these hide things like rocks and tree roots that are best when hit straight on, versus at a glancing blow. Basically, the more you turn, the higher your chances of having your front end deflect off of something."

Guy Cooper—"If your bike is water-cooled, make sure you have a good set of radiator guards that offer side protection. This is the best way to prevent damage in case you smack a tree."

Ty Davis—"I'll use a brake snake [a piece of cable run from the brake pedal to the frame] in the woods to keep the rear brake pedal from getting damaged."

Larry Roeseler—"I always like to use heavy-duty inner tubes when riding around tree roots, because they can cause flats just as easily as rocks."

Sand, by contrast, absorbs a lot of energy. That's why you can jump higher when you know you'll be landing on a surface that provides a cushioning effect.

Rocks force most forks to deflect rather than absorb the impact. That's why many professional riders agree that the best approach is to use finesse. Muscling your way though a rock bed is a surefire way to get hurt.

In most instances, the best approach is to stand and carry your body weight slightly rear of center. This lightens the front-end weight slightly, which means the suspension can work more effectively. The rearward weighting enables the front wheel and fork to bounce off obstacles without as much disruption.

"Try not to tense up when you're riding in rocks," Ty Davis recommends. "This is probably the most common problem, because most people are extremely fearful of crashing and therefore ride extremely rigid. Though it may seem difficult at first, allow the bike to work beneath you. If you let them work, most bikes will do a decent job of riding over rocks."

Technique is also based on line choice. In general, it's much easier to travel straight through a rock bed than meander. When turning the bike, the front wheel can deflect off the rocks, and you can crash your brains out. Just ride straight!

The best path is typically the shortest, but it all depends on rock size. In most cases, stay away from larger rocks, which can damage you and your bike. If you must ride near rocks at footpeg height or higher, Davis suggests riding "with your toes facing upwards. You can't believe how many people break their feet and their toes by smacking into things they 'didn't see.' "

Rock shape is important, too. Sharp, jagged-edged rocks are prone to cause flats, and round rocks are generally more slippery—you have to be the judge and predict how your bike will react. Wet rocks are usually the worst,

Typically, the best approach through rock beds is standing up, with your weight centered on the bike. Choose the smoothest line and avoid wheelspin, which will usually send the rear wheel into a pinball-like state. Once the rear wheel starts bouncing from side to side, it's difficult to regain control.

Look out for hidden rocks. This 250-pound boulder was covered in moss and nestled behind a leaf-covered branch. Nonetheless, it breaks everything it comes in contact with.

because traction is almost nonexistent.

Because traction is a prevailing problem, many rock specialists avoid excess wheelspin and stay off the clutch. Instead, they let torque work them through a rock bed.

While standing is the preferred method, sitting can be an effective way to negotiate fairly even rock beds at slow speeds. Sitting can help provide traction to the rear wheel on inclines, and it enables you to lift your feet off the footpegs, to avoid rocks that have the potential to break your feet.

You do, however, have to be careful with foot placement. Both feet should be kept on the footpegs at all times, unless you're forced to dab or miss a rock. Anytime you take a foot off the peg, you generally lose some of your ability to help the suspension soak up impact, because your knees are almost useless unless used together.

Dabbing in rocks is also dangerous, because usually the only times you're forced to dab are in areas of larger rocks. The larger rocks make it more difficult to find a place to

drop your foot, because it's easy for it to deflect off a rock at speed and cause it to go in a direction you don't want it to go. The results can be painful and can damage knees, among other things. However, if you pay close attention, you can survive.

Water Crossings

Water crossings are one of the most mysterious elements in off-road riding, because of the secrets water hides beneath the surface. Rocks, tree roots, mud, sand, and even depth itself make water crossing extremely challenging most of the time.

The most important aspect is evaluating the situation. First, you have to make sure the body of water is in fact crossable, which may not always be easy to tell. This is where your judgment comes into play. If you're unsure, try walking across, or simply look for an alternative line or turn back.

Another determining factor is current. If the water is moving swiftly, you could easily

ROCKS

- **Look for the smoothest line.**
- **Watch for bowling-ball-size rocks that could hit your footpeg and injure your feet.**
- **Watch out for hidden rocks.**
- **Stay focused and avoid being overly aggressive.**
- **Avoid wheelspin.**
- **Make sure your bike is protected with guards.**
- **Watch for sharp rocks that could cause flats.**
- **Try to keep your feet on the footpegs as much as possible.**

If you find a line that's smooth enough where you feel comfortable sitting down, you still have to remain alert. In this turn, Ty Davis discovers that it's best to stay seated, because it would be too difficult to lift his left leg over the rock while standing. He raises his leg as high as possible without interfering with the handlebar.

ROCKS

Guy Cooper—"Use as many guards as possible to prevent damage to your bike. The last thing you need is a rock breaking your center cases or bending your rear rotor."

Ty Davis—"When I know that it's going to be real rocky, I will use a brake snake. A brake snake is a small cable that attaches from the brake pedal to the frame, to prevent the brake pedal from being severely damaged if it were to encounter a rock."

Dick Burleson—"You really need to be light on the bike and let the front end go where it wants. You can't force the bike in rocks—you have to guide it. You also want to ride cautiously, but don't go too slow. Remember, your suspension needs a little speed to allow it to work properly."

Guy Cooper—"In rocky areas, I always use a steering stabilizer. I also find steering stabilizers useful for high speeds and have even used them in outdoor motocross."

Ty Davis—"Most of the time I recommend using heavy-duty inner tubes, even if you don't expect to encounter rocks. A flat tire will waste time on the trail."

Dick Burleson—"Rocks, tree roots, and the rest of the nasty stuff is what separates the men from the boys. When you find a trick rock section, practice it over and over until you feel comfortable."

Guy Cooper—"If it's really rocky I will use a [bib] mousse, so that I'm 100 percent certain that I won't get a flat tire. That way, you can ride as aggressively as you want without any fear of tire failure."

Larry Roeseler—"I use a shark fin to protect the rear rotor. The shark fin replaces the standard plastic rotor cover found on most bikes and is nearly impossible to bend."

Ken Faught—"I'm a big fan of steering stabilizers. They allow you to adjust tension on the front end, so you can have one setting for tree roots, another for slow-speed turns, and another for rocks. Steering stabilizers are one of the best-kept secrets in off-road riding."

Guy Cooper—"When riding in rocks, I use bark busters to protect the levers in case I fall. You don't waste time changing levers on the trail."

get knocked off your bike and put yourself in serious danger. Many riders underestimate the power of current. If you're concerned, don't try it.

If you determine that the water is safe to cross, pick the shallowest, most direct route and proceed slowly, so you don't splash water into your air box. The best method is to stand with your weight centered, so you can be prepared in case you sink into a hole or the bike hits a rock or another hidden obstacle.

"If there are too many rocks, you may want to consider walking your bike across," suggests Tommy Norton. "This will reduce the risk of cutting a tire on underground rocks. You also have to watch out for underwater ruts in places used by a lot of riders."

If the crossing isn't too deep, Guy Cooper has a recommendation. "When I know the water is fairly shallow and doesn't have any rocks, I'll sit on the seat and lift my legs as high up as possible, to keep my boots from getting soaked. Moisture is one of the main causes of blistering, plus it's not a whole lot of fun riding in wet boots."

Cooper also has an answer for small crossings, for really experienced riders. "If the stream is really narrow, you may consider wheelying across. This will decrease water spray, which could spoil your goggles, plus you don't have to worry about hitting any hidden rocks that could cause your front end to twist."

Log Crossings

Fallen trees can be intimidating, especially the larger ones. Things like ground clearance, traction, and gravity sometimes make it seem impossible to get over such an obstacle, let alone in total control. When no alternative lines are available and you don't want to turn back, a couple of techniques are commonly used.

The most popular is the ultra-low-speed wheelie approach. This is where riders use careful throttle and clutch control to loft the front tire over the log, all the while making sure the rear end doesn't slam into the other side and get stuck momentarily. Furthermore, the goal is to avoid rear wheelspin, so the back of the bike can get as much traction as possible,

Crossing Water

Before crossing any body of water, make sure you have a good idea of the depth. Though it's not easy to gauge, strive for the shallowest point to make your crossing. Wheelying across can be a good way to keep dry, but the resistance of the water will pull the front end down. Also, be certain that the bottom of the river is relatively smooth—a hidden log or rock could give you a quick trip over the bars and into the drink.

WATER

- **Look for the shortest and shallowest place to cross.**
- **Stand up, so you can use your knees to compensate for any sudden changes in terrain.**
- **Be alert for underwater rocks that could affect steering.**
- **Make sure your electrical system is properly sealed.**
- **Don't create so much splashing that water gets into your air filter.**

lofting the front wheel while the rear wheel is in contact with the tree's surface.

This approach must be undertaken at slow speeds, or you may not be able to get the front end high enough—and if you do, the rear end will rebound so fast that it will probably cause you to go over the handlebar. This approach generally requires a straight shot at the obstacle, because hitting the downed tree at an angle will only cause the rear wheel to slide. (The exception to this rule consists of areas along the trunk that have V-shaped crevices formed by broken tree limbs. These crevices help keep your back end in line with the front end and make conquering trees much less challenging.)

After choosing your point of contact, initiate a small wheelie. Stand up, weight the back of your bike, and use enough throttle and clutch to get the front wheel high enough to

safely clear the tree. Don't overdo it, or you may lose too much momentum once the rear wheel strikes the side of the log. If you place it perfectly, the front wheel will kiss the top of the log. If you don't get the wheel high enough, you may find yourself tossed over the bars.

Once the front wheel is safely over, prepare to absorb some of the impact with your knees and elbows. Push away on the handlebar to redirect the momentum forward, and be prepared to suck the bike up to your inseam. In some cases, you may be forced to momentarily chop the throttle, but if you do, make sure you aren't overly aggressive when reapplying power. Wheelspin, especially if the log is covered in moss, will make the bike much more difficult to control.

Once the rear tire is on top of the log, you should be in good shape. Remain standing until both wheels have touched the ground.

WATER CROSSINGS

Ty Davis—"Make sure that your entire electrical system is sealed properly—otherwise, your engine could quit rather abruptly. When this happens it will take you forever to get it started again."

Guy Cooper—"Use a good skid plate to protect your engine cases from rock damage."

Dick Burleson—"Water is very tricky, because you can't see what's beneath you. This is one of the rare cases where it's important to go slow. But don't go so slow that you will get stuck. It all depends on the conditions, but water crossings in general can be very tricky."

Ty Davis—"Seal the air box really tightly, so that water can't get inside the engine. I usually take the entire air box apart and seal all of the joints with silicone. If there are any holes on the side, you should cover them up with duct tape."

Dick Burleson—"Try to figure out water depth before trying to cross. If you don't have a good idea of depth, don't think about crossing."

Shane Watts—"Scout the riding area and look for the shallowest point. Water can be very deceiving, and it's better to go slower than banzai straight through."

Ken Faught—"Use hand guards when you think you might need to ride through water. This will help keep your grips and gloves dry. I also carry an extra pair of gloves if I plan on riding in the wet, because wet gloves can cause your hands to blister very quickly."

Log Crossings

1. Getting over downed trees is tough but not impossible. When all else fails, it may be necessary to lift the bike over. The easiest method is to get the front wheel over first, rest the bike on the lower frame rails, then lift the back end over.

2. This small log can be easily crossed with the wheelie technique. By normal means it would be unrideable, because hitting it front-wheel first would be the equivalent of running into a short brick wall. The wheelie approach, though tricky, is the method preferred by top riders. It requires perfect timing, good judgment, and excellent control. The idea is to ride up to the log at low speed and loft the front wheel over it. If you hit the log too fast, your rear wheel will kick up as the rear suspension rebounds, throwing you over the bars. *Karel Kramer*

3. This log is much larger and requires more throttle and clutch control. Remember that the larger the log, the slower the speed. The idea is to loft the front end high enough to clear the log—but not too high, or it'll be more difficult to control once the bike makes contact. As the rear wheel hits, the bike will want to kick the back end up and throw the front end down. The effects of speed on the suspension increase the faster you go—hence the importance of slowing down to just a few miles per hour.

Crossing Angled Logs

1. This log is approximately 8 inches in diameter, but it can still wreak havoc with suspension. The wheelie approach is also used extensively on obstacles this size. Sometimes, however, you may be forced to hit the log at an angle, which usually causes the back end to slide out almost instantaneously and send you and your bike crashing to the ground. One trick riders commonly use is to find a V-shaped spot on the tree to firmly plant the rear wheel before wheeling. This makes angled logs much easier to conquer.

2. Eight-time ISDE Gold Medalist Dick Burleson hits this log at a 45-degree angle. As his rear wheel hits the log, his tire will instantly deflect, causing the bike to want to slide. Burleson reduces his speed and tries to be as smooth as possible with his body and throttle position, to prevent unsettling the motorcycle even further. *Karel Kramer*

LOG CROSSINGS

- **Look for the lowest point to cross.**
- **Loft the front wheel over, and ease the rear across at low speed.**
- **Avoid wheelspin.**
- **Watch out for broken branches.**
- **Look for alternative lines.**
- **Get your riding buddies to help you lift your bike over if it's too difficult to ride over.**

The second approach to log crossing is sheer body strength. After you can no longer ride the bike, it becomes necessary to lift it over. The easiest method is to use the bike's power to lift the front wheel up and over the top of the log. This can be done sitting, standing, or even with your body off the bike, standing to the side. The idea is to use careful throttle and clutch control to loft the front wheel from a dead stop and then place it on top of the log, preferably resting the bike on its engine cases.

From there, all you have to do is lift the back end of the bike over. It's not going to be the easiest thing you'll ever do, but it won't be as heavy as lifting the entire bike over. If it becomes too challenging, ask some of your riding buddies to help.

Regardless of which technique you use, watch out for items such as sharp tree limbs or leaf-covered branches that could cause injury. You want an unobstructed path around the area of the tree you intend to conquer.

"Practice on smaller logs and then work your way up to ones that are larger," Ty Davis recommends. "Remember, the bigger they are, the slower you have to go, because of the way your suspension will react."

"Try to avoid logs on downhills, because they're much harder to wheelie over, and it makes it really tough to control the bike," adds Guy Cooper. "Generally you'll

Speed can be tons of fun, but it must be respected. A few simple modifications, such as the steering stabilizer attached to the lower triple clamp, can make the bike more stable at warp nine. Sliding the forks lower in the triple clamps, which extends rake, can also help stabilize the bike.

hit the log too fast, and it will want to throw you over the bars."

While it may be easier to wheelie uphill, it's more difficult to overcome downed trees, because it affects your momentum more

severely. An obvious idea is to attack it faster, but this will only cause your suspension to rebound much faster than would normally be considered safe. About the only thing you can do is get the front wheel up and over, then

Flat terrain can produce incredibly high speeds, but it can also instill overconfidence. No matter how fast you're going, be extremely alert and know your surroundings. *Joe Bonnello*

search for as much traction as possible in hopes of getting the rear wheel to follow.

Using these techniques a couple times should give you a good idea of how your bike will react.

Dealing with Speed

How fast is fast? To some riders, it's 40 miles an hour on a rutted straight on a motocross track. To others, it's full throttle at 100 miles an hour down the Mexican peninsula in Baja. Regardless of the actual miles per hour, top riders employ several tricks when speeds get higher than normal.

The most important factor is the terrain and conditions. It's imperative not to exceed a safe speed, or you put yourself in serious jeopardy. Make sure you have plenty of room to brake for upcoming obstacles. This means you have to be looking far enough ahead to see changes in the terrain. Never assume something is safe just because it looks tame. Something as small as a 1-inch-deep rain rut can spell disaster if you're traveling at warp speed.

Also be alert for two-way traffic. Even though you may have enough time to avoid fixed obstacles, don't forget about moving targets, such as other riders or even the surrounding wildlife. Many off-road riders have

run into animals—in fact, even motocrossers aren't immune. Multi-time World Champion Greg Albertyn hit a deer while racing a Grand Prix motocross race. It knocked him off his bike and nearly landed him in the hospital.

"Always be alert," says Guy Cooper. "Most accidents happen when riders become overconfident."

At speed, it's also important to pay strict attention to body position. You generally want to weight the rear of the bike, because this tends to reduce headshake while allowing the suspension to work more effectively. Many experts also relax their grip on the handlebar, so the front end can twitch naturally. Many riders find that if they're tense, they can actually induce a high-speed wobble.

If a high-speed wobble (also known as headshake) does occur, the rule of thumb is to get on the throttle as quickly as possible, to help take a load off the front suspension. You can also lightly apply the rear brake. The worst thing you can do is slam on the front brake, which will worsen the headshake. Of course, if a dangerous obstacle lies ahead, you may have to take your chances and get on the brakes as much as necessary.

Even if everything is going smoothly, it's always a good idea to keep your fingers on the

clutch and brake levers and your foot next to the brake pedal at all times. This speed up your reaction time in case you have to slow down abruptly.

Sidehills and Off-Cambers

Hills and mountains pose many challenges. One of the most unusual involves off-cambers and the fine art known as sidehilling. This technique is used extensively for traveling across the face of the hill. When you find yourself staring at a gnarly grade you have to cross, your sidehilling technique will be put to the test.

The trick with sidehilling is to avoid losing altitude. As you cross the hill, the slope and the force of gravity make your bike tend to slide down the hill.

Another problem is finding traction. As with an off-camber, the sloped surface of the hill will leave the outside edge of your knobbies digging in air. With traction reduced, you're more likely to slide and are less able to turn and accelerate.

Proper sidehilling always begins with careful analysis of the situation. You must know exactly where you're going and how you're going to get there. You have to look at the terrain type, keeping in mind that sand, snow, loose rock, and mud make it nearly impossible to sidehill. Also look for other obstacles, such as boulders, logs, tree branches, and anything else that may disrupt your travel.

If you can, stop and spend a little time planning a line before you tackle the sidehill. Choose an ideal line and pick some likely alternates, to give yourself some options. Don't plan to fail, but if you see a particularly tough spot, have an escape route in mind if

DEALING WITH SPEED

Ty Davis—"Most riders will use a steering stabilizer when speeds get really high. It will take some of the nervousness out of the front end. Steering stabilizers inspire confidence and are a good investment."

Shane Watts—"Gearing is really important, especially when you're trying to maintain that speed for a long time. In most cases, it's best to lower your revs by running a taller gear. This is a cheap way to help your motor last longer, but it will hurt acceleration."

Guy Cooper—"One of the easiest ways to make your bike handle better at speed is to lower the fork in the triple clamp, so that the top of the tubes are flush with the top of the clamp. This will extend the wheelbase, which should reduce headshake."

Ty Davis—"If you're racing, try to pre-run the course. This will give you a good chance to learn the area and also check gearing. If your bike is geared too low, you risk blowing the engine up, and you'll lose valuable time."

Ken Faught—"I always try to stretch the wheelbase out as much as possible. I'll run a longer chain to get the rear wheel as far back as possible in the swingarm."

Looking ahead at obstacles is important. These two boulders could cause serious bodily harm, but Faught saw them early enough to adjust his riding technique. He's taken both feet off the pegs, so his feet don't get smashed. He uses his legs to push himself forward and keep his weight as far forward as possible, to prevent looping out.

you get off-line. And don't try it if dire consequences lie below.

"Never try to cross over an area above a cliff," adds Ty Davis. "It's important to always have a path down the hill in case you can't make it all the way across."

When possible, look for pre-existing lines that travel across the face of the hill. These are important, especially on extreme angles, because they'll help keep your wheels in line. If you're crossing virgin soil, you'll spend most of the trip fighting the bike.

Maintain as straight a path as possible, weight the outside footpeg for balance, maintain momentum without any sudden bursts of power, and make relatively few gear changes. Also, stay off the brakes, because they'll usually cause you to lose traction and start slipping down.

"If you have to brake, it's usually better to use the rear," says Mike Healey. "If you grab a handful of front brake, the front wheel may wash out. That's why it's usually best to slow down by simply backing off the throttle and coasting to a stop. If you have to use the brakes, do so very carefully. Apply each one smoothly and slowly, so you don't affect the handling."

Of the two wheels, the front is perhaps the most important, because it dictates where

SIDEHILLING

- Look for the smoothest line.
- Avoid excessive speed.
- Weight the outside footpeg.
- Make sure you know where the trail leads.
- Avoid sidehilling near cliffs.
- Look for the most traction.
- Use ruts or pre-existing lines to your advantage.
- Avoid sharp turns.
- Maintain momentum.
- Avoid quick bursts of power that produce excessive wheelspin.

the bike is intended to go—and wherever the front wheel goes, the rear usually follows.

Sidehilling can be done sitting or standing, although sitting is usually preferred, because it lowers the center of gravity. Then again, standing is sometimes necessary, especially if you approach an obstacle that will disrupt your suspension.

If no lines are available and virgin terrain is your only option, devote total concentration to your route. If the back wheel starts to slide, add more weight to the outside footpeg. In some instances, you may have to get on the throttle a little, but don't overdo it, or the bike will most likely dig in if the soil is soft.

If you're forced to cross sand, snow, or other loose terrain at an angle, you may have to allow the rear end to drop out of line with the front wheel. This technique requires more power than normal but is effective. Essentially, this is similar to what pilots do to combat strong winds.

Regardless of terrain type, Bob Hannah says you should "always look far enough ahead so that you have time to change direction in case you see a rain rut or something else blocking your path."

"Pay attention to any changes in terrain that could affect traction," says Davis. "If you're going from hardpack to sand, you'll probably

have to give the bike a little more gas to maintain your momentum. If the opposite occurs and you go from sand to hardpack, you probably need to back off the throttle a little bit, so the wheel doesn't spin."

"If you're going downhill and decide you want to sidehill across, the easiest way to get your bike lined up in the direction you want is to brake-slide the rear end and then gently roll on the throttle once you get pointed the right way," suggests Rick Sowma. "You need to be smooth, though. It'll be difficult to slow down because of the momentum, and you could high-side once you get the bike totally sideways."

"If you have to get off your bike because you can no longer keep going, it's best to get off on the high side," recommends Davis. "This

will give you much more control over the bike and will make sure the bike doesn't fall on top of you in case you have any big problems."

"Don't follow too close to other riders, because if they have problems, you may have a difficult time getting around them," adds Healey, "Especially if they're lying on the ground."

Downhills: Nature's Express Lane

On uphills, the challenge is making it to the top. On downhills, one wrong move and both rider and bike find that gravity offers an instant and unforgiving express lane to the bottom. That's precisely why most riders have a love/hate relationship with big descents. When conditions are

Downhill 101

1. Downhills can be loads of fun when done correctly. Watch out for acceleration and braking bumps, which can upset suspension.

right, downhills can be a blast. But when terrain and/or weather turn nasty, downhills can be brutal and downright scary.

Most problems surround the difficulty of stopping. Momentum builds quickly, depending on the severity of the angle, making it tough to reduce speed. Downhills also require careful body positioning and limited throttle use, which wreak havoc with suspension. That's because most suspension is set up to be balanced when your body weight is centered.

On downhills, the preferred body position is toward the back, but the slope of the hill forces most of the (motorcycle and body) weight onto the fork. Under braking, the fork is bearing almost all the weight. With the fork near the bottom of the stroke, little travel is available, and damping is harsh. Stutter bumps, hard braking, and an extreme downhill are a good recipe for an endo.

The best way to alleviate this effect is to accelerate, which takes some weight off the fork and puts it on the rear suspension. Under acceleration, your front end will rise a bit and will be able to soak up rugged terrain much more effectively. Of course, you can't go down the entire length of most slopes at full throttle, so you want to accelerate hardest through the rough spots.

Downhills also toy with the rear suspension, but in an entirely different manner. With most of the weight on the front fork, the rear end of the motorcycle becomes extremely light, which is why it's easy to endo. Steep downhills lighten the weight on the rear suspension, making the bike ride higher in the rear and the brake action less effective. The result is that your rear brake has little or no stopping power, and the rear end will kick up easily.

With your bike unbalanced, pay special attention to the terrain. In a lot of cases, you'll occasionally have to accelerate hard over a bump, rock, hole, stump, log, tree branch, or what have you, just to get the front suspension to work properly. Although this is an aggressive approach, it's effective.

Before you attempt a downhill, it's crucial to have a safe plan mapped out in your head. Motocross or other closed-course riders have the luxury of taking it slow a couple of times or even walking the hill beforehand (which is highly recommended). For off-road riders, downhills can be much more

2. This shot of Guy Cooper clearly shows the effect that downhill braking has on suspension. The fork is deep into the travel, while the rear end is higher than normal.

3. The rear brake is vital on downhills and is typically applied whenever the front brake is in use. Many riders also use the rear binders to brake-slide around turns. Here, Guy Cooper's brake is activated with only slight pedal movement. If the pedal were lower, it would be difficult to use effectively, because of the body positioning required for riding downhill.

the rear brake will slow you down a bit. You can also use a technique skiers use to descend: traversing from side to side, so you drop at a slower rate. (See the Sidehill section for proper body position.) Pay attention to the terrain and look for areas that offer the most traction. Traction usually translates into control, which is essential when you're on the side of a steep incline.

If there's one thing to remember about downhills, it's to take your time. It's difficult to emphasize how fast things happen while descending, and the penalties can be quick and severe.

Uphills and Cliff Climbs: A Higher Learning

Uphills are one of the few obstacles where technique alone won't always provide success. Though good technique is required for extremely steep terrain, the buzzword around hill climbs is usually power, and lots of it. Displacement pays off big, especially on steep grades, which is why big-bore bikes haven't slipped into extinction. Cubic centimeters aren't, however, the only factor when it comes to success. Effective riding technique can make up for the lack of displacement.

Cliff climbs also rely on power, but success usually depends more on technique, finesse, and confidence. In many ways, cliff climbs have a lot in common with uphills, but there are some important differences.

dangerous. It's not uncommon to ride into a dead end, with no safe or rideable way down. Rock outcroppings can trick you into thinking something is safe when it actually leads to a 150-foot vertical cliff with no way to turn around.

If you're riding in a new area, walking the downhill may be your best bet. And if you don't think you can make it, walking or "bulldogging" the bike down is the safest route.

When traveling downhill, it's also wise

not to follow another rider too closely or have a rider on your tail. If something happens to one of you, it could get ugly in a hurry.

Ruts add another nasty element to downhills. They can be good when turning on sidehills, but make sure you don't get cross-rutted, or it will be difficult to regain control, especially if you're on a steep angle.

If you're worried about building too much speed and the effects of using the front brake,

Downhill Jumps

Even small descents such as this one mandate placing your weight toward the rear of the bike. Larry Roeseler is jumping off the top, but he still has to land on a downward angle. Though it looks as though he's sitting, he's actually standing in a crouched position and will remain standing until he reaches flat ground. The theory behind most downhill jumps is to match the angle of the bike with the terrain. In this case, Roeseler has let the front drop more than usual for a reason. He wants to get the front wheel on the ground as soon as possible, to begin his braking.

Pick a Route

The first order of business is to examine the hill or cliff for an unobstructed route to the top. The idea is to avoid rocks, logs, tree branches, deep ruts, or anything else that could throw you off balance and rob you of momentum. When examining the situation, search for the easiest way to the top.

"Look for the straightest route up the hill and an area that's the least vertical," says Danny Hamel. "Most of the time, it'll be necessary to weave from side to side to follow preexisting lines, but always attempt the straightest shot possible. . . . Your tires will work more effectively."

Terrain is also important. Sand soaks up a lot of momentum, and rocks provide minimal traction. Along with mud and snow, all four of these elements will make your climb more difficult.

Building Speed

Once you've chosen the best route, build as much momentum as you feel is necessary. Balance speed with impact and simple common sense. If the hill starts gradually, without an abrupt face, and is relatively open, you can hit it in a higher gear. If the hill has a sudden slope at the base or is strewn with trees, rocks, ruts, or other obstacles, your attack speed with have to be lower.

In general, more speed is better. A hill puts more strain on your engine, and it's difficult, although not impossible, to build more speed as you climb. Your only real option is to downshift as you go. On big-bore machines you may not have to, but smaller bikes are likely to run out of beans as you climb.

Body Position and Traction

When you hit the base of the hill, stay loose and in the attack position. As you climb, you'll need to move forward and backward to keep the rear wheel hooked up and the front end from wheelying. On most climbs, you'll need to adjust your body position to maintain traction. When the rear wheel breaks loose and spins, move your hips to the rear of the bike for more bite. If the bike wheelies, slide forward and lean over the bars, to bring the front end down. If that isn't enough to stop the wheelie, slip the clutch to lower the front wheel rather than backing off the throttle.

Danny Hamel explains how he maintains good traction on uphills. "On hills that don't offer a lot of traction, it's good to sit as far back as possible to weight the rear end. As traction becomes more available and causes the bike to wheelie, you need to shift your weight further forward. You'll always find you're constantly searching for the correct seat position."

"I think a lot of people underestimate how important it is to stand up when attacking an uphill," says eight-time Great American Hill-climb Champion Travis Whitlock. "A lot of people feel you need to lean forward over the bike, when in fact you want to stand on your pegs with your weight transferred to the rear wheel, so the bike will hook up. If the hill has big bumps, kickers, or ledges, you're better off standing, so your legs can absorb a lot of the shock, and then use the clutch to keep the front end light.

"To me, the secret to hillclimbing is maintaining momentum and using the clutch. You need to find that fine line between

Uphills are an incredible test of rider skill and machine capability, especially when they're slippery and littered with rocks and boulders. They can be intimidating, but once overcome, they also reward you with a sense of accomplishment. Here, *Dirt Rider*'s Ken Faught tries to maintain forward momentum, to avoid wheelspin that could stop him in his tracks. *Karel Kramer*

edly, while simultaneously shifting your weight back and forth.

Take a Seat

On a smooth approach, you can attack the hill sitting down, as Ty Davis attests. "Unless tackling an obstacle that will disrupt your suspension, usually you should be in the seated position, but exactly where depends on a lot of factors. The idea is to maintain traction by sitting over the rear wheel. However, this can cause the bike to wheelie.

"Most of the time, the best body position for climbing steep hills is to be seated, with your body weight forward, to keep the bike from wheelying. It's basically the attack position. This way, if you need to stand for any reason, like to jump over a rain rut or hit a small jump, you can raise up pretty quickly and absorb a lot of the impact with your legs. On more gradual hills, sometimes standing is preferred, especially if there are a lot of acceleration bumps."

Smooth Power

Throughout the entire length of the uphill, power delivery must be smooth. For starters, select the proper gear at the bottom, which will put you in the meat of the powerband. In most situations it's difficult to upshift, so downshifting is your only true option.

Avoid excessive clutch work to build power. Every time you slip the clutch to build revs, you'll most likely spin the tire and dig in,

wheelying and keeping your speed up. When you lose momentum and have to use the clutch too much, the bike will want to wheelie when you apply power. When this happens, you either have to get out of the power or use the clutch some more, and that only amplifies

the wheelying problem, which either causes you to flip over or dig in."

Regardless, no single technique is correct; it all depends on the situation. To achieve the right balance in some instances, you may find you have to sit and stand repeat-

G-Outs

1. G-outs occur when you're faced with a landing at the bottom of a jump or incline that bottoms your suspension and hammers your body. Ty Davis shows how to handle the big hit. To most riders, this fourth-gear downhill would pose an interesting dilemma, because of the drop-off at the bottom. Worse, the landing zone is a sand wash, which robs loads of momentum on impact. While some riders would instinctively brake hard to lessen the force of the landing, Davis decides to carry the front wheel high off the jump.

2. The impact bottoms Davis' rear suspension hard, but he's able to minimize the blow, because the landing area allows him to stay on the throttle. The throttle continues the forward motion and helps his bike track straight in the sand. Fast deceleration in sand on this type of obstacle would normally be tricky and dangerous.

which can rob you of momentum. The clutch can, however, serve an effective role.

"On really steep uphills, if the bike starts to wheelie and you're already sitting as far forward as possible, you should slip the clutch a little instead of backing off the throttle," Hamel says. "If you back off the throttle too much, it'll be difficult to build rpm without a lot of clutch work. Whatever you do, you want to stay off the brakes unless absolutely necessary."

Bailing Out

If you do feel you can't make it to the top of the hill and there's no safe way to sidehill, it's usually best to back off the throttle, apply both brakes, and prepare to lean the bike over to one side. Some riders try to ride it out to the very end and believe they haven't given their best effort until they've looped their bike. After it's done cartwheeling 200 feet downhill, bending the bars, the radiators, and both levers and ruining the plastic, they realize it may not have been the best approach.

Once you're forced to stop, try to get your bike perpendicular to the trail and step off the high side. Seldom do you want to have the bike above you on a hill, because it's much more difficult to control and is more likely to fall on you.

Cliff climbs are similar, but they're usually much shorter and based more on rider style.

"For cliff climbing, it's usually best to stand up from start to finish," says Guy Cooper. "This will allow your body to absorb a lot of the shock that occurs as the bike goes vertical almost instantly. Sometimes the impact will cause the bike to bottom, almost like a G-out, and you need to be prepared.

"Watch out for rocks, tree roots or anything else that could cause your wheels to deflect as you climb up any cliff, because you can't afford to lose traction," adds Cooper. "Watch for ruts, too. They could knock your feet off the footpegs, which will kill your momentum. Remember, most cliffs are very unforgiving."

"Before you climb any cliff, make sure you know what's on the other side," Davis says. "I've seen guys do some cliff jumps where they think the top is a plateau, when it's actually a drop-off."

"Don't follow other riders up cliff jumps, because if they screw up, it'll be almost impossible for you to make it to the top," says Rick Sowma. "It's usually easier to make it to the top when you don't have to dodge the rider and cartwheeling bike."

"If you feel you're not going to successfully complete a cliff climb, it's usually best to jump off the bike to the side," adds Sowma. "This way, your body should hit the face of the cliff and be able to use its traction to break your fall to the base of the cliff. You also want to get away from the bike, so it doesn't land on you or you don't land on it."

If and when you make it to the top, you'll have to lower the front end fairly quickly, because the bike may be nearly vertical. The best way is to push down on the handlebar and add weight to the front of the bike. But you don't want to go overboard, or you could endo. It's vital to stay on the gas once you land, so you can power away from the cliff. Throttle application will also help your suspension absorb some of the impact.

G-Outs: Taking the Big Hit

A G-out is an extremely hard landing that bottoms the bike's suspension and jars the rider's body. It's a shock that generates enough G-force to exceed all the absorbing characteristics of the suspension components.

Though there are many ways to totally bottom a bike, a G-out usually results from an obstacle where forward motion is interrupted by an abrupt incline. Sometimes this can

G-OUTS

- Adjust your body weight so it's slightly rear of center.
- Slowing down usually softens the impact.
- Keep your toes pointed up, so if you bottom, your feet won't get hung up on anything lying on the ground.
- Stand whenever you hit a G-out, so your legs and arms soak up some of the impact.

include other obstacles, such as a jump, water crossing, or rain rut, but rarely are G-outs something riders enjoy.

"G-outs are always tricky, because you don't know the severity of the impact," Ty Davis says. "Always be cautious, and the first time you hit it, it's usually a good idea to go a little slower than normal, so you know what effect it'll have on your suspension."

Analysis is usually the most important part in taking on this obstacle. Because you already anticipate harsh bottoming, look for a location that's the least severe. Also watch for rocks, rain ruts, or weird variations in terrain that could further hamper your handling. Since your suspension will most likely fully collapse, your engine cases will be lower to the ground, and a rock could damage your cases even if you have a skid plate. Furthermore, your tires will fully compress, and chances are good that when this happens in a rocky area, you could get a flat and/or ding the rim.

Once you've committed, do all your braking beforehand. If you slam into the other side with the brake on, it will only slow your momentum more quickly.

In almost every instance, the preferred body position is standing, with your weight

Off-Road Ruts

1. Rut-riding is a skill that takes a lot of time to develop. Even world-class riders such as Dick Burleson find that each new rut offers a multitude of new challenges. This line, for example, is blanketed with vines, tree roots, and downed branches. This is one of the rare cases where you may want to remove your feet from the footpegs. In this picture, the rut is so deep that Burleson is forced to dismount and muscle his bike over the rise.

slightly rear of center. This allows your knees and elbows to help absorb the impact.

It's also usually better to carry the front wheel a little high, so that the shock can take the hit first and then transfer some of the remaining energy to the fork. To further reduce the harshness, it's common for riders to give the bike gas, to help maintain momentum.

Uphill Ruts: Momentum Is Your Best Friend

Riding uphill is difficult when there are no ruts to worry about. A steep incline is a sure test of talent, since proper body position, clutch use, and throttle control become critical to maintaining traction. If you lean too far forward, you have a good chance of wheelspin. If you lean too far backward, the bike is likely to wheelie and possibly loop out. You have to worry about all this while dodging trees, rocks, and other obstacles.

The introduction of ruts drastically increases the difficulty of uphills, no matter how long or how steep. It causes even the most experienced riders plenty of grief, because it usually means line choice is extremely limited.

In recreational riding and in racing, ruts form on the best or only line. In many cases, ruts develop at the bottom of single-track trails and/or any inside line, affecting your momentum.

During most encounters with ruts, you won't have many options. Though you can look for alternative lines on the outskirts of the trail, in most cases a better one is hard to come by.

Just as in normal uphills, momentum is critical. It's hard to accelerate quickly once you've begun your ascent. It's much more desirable to build speed before the hill, because, in most cases, ruts brush off more speed than they help create.

Ruts are only as good as the people who make them. If the line wanders from side to side, it's because the original riders who dug the line had difficulty going straight. The same theory holds true for turns at the base of uphills. If the line isn't smooth (perhaps it requires squaring off), it's typically the first rider's fault.

Sometimes a single rut branches out into a series of ruts, which provides several options. Pay attention to what's happening up ahead, so you can make quick decisions.

2. At the base of this hill, Guy Cooper looks for an alternative line and finds it less than half a foot from a group of ruts. To use the line, he has to skirt to the extreme outside but finds that his new line offers better drive to the awaiting uphill. As you can see, his line offers a straight shot, unlike the groove he's avoiding—which has a slight bend, but enough to brush off speed.

3. One of the fundamental principles of hill climbing and rut riding is to keep your feet on the footpegs as much as possible. Any dab will cause you to lose momentum. Dabbing is usually the result of poor body position combined with a sudden handlebar correction. Typically, you want to keep your body weight centered over the bike. In this photo, Cooper is leaning way to the side, and his bike has started to wheelie. He's lost almost all his momentum. Before long, he'll have to start paddling with his feet to correct the situation.

"Look for a way out if you don't like where your rut is heading," Ty Davis recommends. "Keep an eye out for a shallow point in the groove that leads to flat ground or a better line."

Momentum is doubly important in ruts, because contact with rut walls brushes off speed in most instances. On the other hand, you have to be careful about the opposite extreme.

"Riding too aggressively in ruts is not a good idea, because it'll force mistakes," Davis says. "You want to flow with the bike as much as possible. Don't tense up, but instead, try to stay loose and fluid."

"Once you start going uphill, try to keep the throttle on as long as possible," adds Guy Cooper. "You lose speed quickly when traveling uphill, and it's difficult to get it back. In most cases, I find it better to slip the clutch momentarily, to slow down, than to get out of the throttle. This way you'll be able to keep up engine rpm more effectively."

Ideally, you should enter the rut with both wheels perfectly lined up with the groove. If one wheel is slightly off, you have a good chance of getting cross rutted. When this happens it's difficult to correct, and if you get both wheels seated, you'll probably have brushed off most of your momentum.

Terrain is also critical. Hardpack is usually good, because excessive wheelspin won't deepen the rut quickly, but it also doesn't offer much traction. Conversely, loam is great for traction, but ruts in soft dirt deteriorate and become unrideable quickly.

In most cases it's preferable to stay seated, because this lowers your center of gravity. This is even more important when traveling uphill, because you need to move forward and backward on the seat in the neverending quest for the right traction. But when a rut becomes too deep, you may have to take your feet off the footpegs and start paddling. Keep your weight as far forward as possible and have your feet near the footpegs, in case you need to shift or stand on the rear brake.

Paddling (sticking your legs out) can work but must be combined with proper throttle application and weight distribution. Riders who get overzealous tend to overrev their bikes, which produces excessive wheelspin. Wheelspin just causes you to dig in, to the point where your rear axle gets hung up on the rut walls and your tire loses contact with the ground.

4. This is an excellent aggressive approach by Guy Cooper. He finds good body positioning and appears to have plenty of momentum.

5. This line has gotten to the point where it's nearly unrideable. It's more than axle deep, causing the swingarm, axle, and footpegs to scrape against the rut walls, brushing off tons of momentum. Cooper is simply trying to ride it out. In actuality, he's unloaded all his weight from the bike and is running with his legs. This puts less strain on the engine and doesn't force the bike deeper into the rut. He's also trying to keep wheelspin to a minimum. Wheelspin will only make the rut deeper, so constant attention must be paid to throttle and clutch control.

6. The rear wheel is almost buried, to the point where the rear sprocket will soon be underground. Cooper is nearly at the crest of the hill, so he's still taking an aggressive approach. The depth of the rut forces him to lean the bike from side to side to get any traction whatsoever. He's also using his own strength to help muscle the bike to the top.

UPHILL RUTS

Guy Cooper—"Make sure that you have a really good chain guide, because it will get really abused if you intend to do a lot of rut riding."

Ty Davis—"Make sure your rim locks are tightened. In really deep ruts, the rear tire will want to spin on the rim, because there is so much normal and sidewall traction."

UPHILL RUTS

- Line up both wheels before the entrance of the rut.
- Avoid wheelspin as much as possible.
- Too much clutch work could make your rear wheel dig in.
- Make sure the rut is not too deep.
- Don't follow other riders too closely.
- Maintain as much momentum as conditions permit.
- Watch for ruts that split into several lines.
- Make sure the rut exits in a desired location.
- Look for alternative lines.
- Watch for rocks, tree roots, or other obstacles protruding from rut walls.
- Avoid being overly aggressive.

If you do get stuck, try rocking your bike from side to side gently (you don't want to bend your rim), then lift it out of the groove. The rocking motion will help free the wheel from the rut.

Trail Survival Tactics

Inevitably, you'll have problems on the trail. It may be a simple mechanical failure, such as a fouled spark plug, or you may get trapped on the side of a hill. Either way it's no fun, and it can spell disaster if you aren't prepared.

Fortunately, you're probably not the first to encounter these problems. Many souls in the past have had trailside problems, and you can benefit from their experience. Here are some of the common problems and solutions:

Getting Lost

If you become lost, seek high ground, so you can search for reference points. If necessary, get off your bike and hike to the top of a hill or mountain. Also, pay attention to the location of the sun—it's usually a good reference point. If you ride in an area that's at all popular, stop your bike and listen for other engines, which can give you an idea of where to head. More important, though, be prepared. Carry a compass and a map, if one is available. Take the time to figure out which direction to head if you get lost, and carry extra gas and water if you're in a large, remote riding area. Last, use your head. If you lose your bearings, stop and survey the situation for a few minutes. Thinking things through is always preferable to charging off half-cocked.

Getting Separated

If you become separated from your group, don't ride off alone unless you're hurt or in danger. Remain in the location where you

Turning Around

1. Just a few feet from the top of this hill, Guy Cooper gets stuck. The rut he's using gets too deep and robs him of all momentum. Though he's basically at the crest, Cooper decides that this is the ideal spot to show how to turn the bike around on a hill. It's a simple survival trick—one you may use often when riding in hilly areas. "The first thing you want to do is get off your bike and keep it from rolling backwards," Cooper says. "Make sure you stand on the side which is the safest and where you feel the most comfortable."

2. "Swing the back end of the motorcycle around by lifting on the fender," Cooper adds. "If you can't lift it all the way off the ground, then just slide it."

3. "Bring the back end around until you sense that it will start rolling down the hill if you go any further." Notice the depth of the rut Cooper's bike is straddling.

last saw other members of your party. In most cases, your buddies will backtrack to find you once they know you're missing.

Spare Tools

Unless you're riding on a motocross track, every member in your group should carry a fanny pack full of tools and spare parts. If you're in a large group, you may be able to consolidate, but tools and spare parts are mandatory.

Food and Drink

Carry some type of liquid and energy bar at all times. Your body needs to be fueled regularly, or it won't function properly. If you have to work hard on the trail, you'll be thankful you planned ahead.

Communications

Advances in technology have made cellular phones inexpensive. If you're riding in a remote location, consider packing a cell phone in case of an emergency.

GPS

Global Positioning Systems cost as little as $100 and can save your life. If you plan on riding long distances away from public roads, this is a great tool to carry in your fanny pack.

Never Ride Alone

Riding with another person is always recommended. If you get stranded or hurt, that person may be the only one who can provide help.

Don't Panic

The most important item to remember in any situation is not to panic. Try to think rationally and determine what you could realistically do to get yourself out of a jam.

Trail Pace

If you don't feel comfortable with the trail pace set by other riders, slow down. If the group is large enough, someone else probably wants to go slower as well. Simply slow your pace and let the others wait for you. If this creates a problem, ask some of the other riders if they want to splinter off the main group and go on a less challenging ride.

4. "Grab onto the handlebar with both hands and begin rocking the bike back and forth, each time turning the bars to get the front end pointing downward. Continue rocking the bike until you have a straight path down the hill. It shouldn't take too long."

5. "While you're moving the bike around, pay attention to your footing. The last thing you want to do is fall over while holding your bike."

6. "As I prepare to remount the bike, I let the bike roll forward, so I can swing my leg over the seat."

7. "With the brakes on, slowly get back on the bike."

8. "Only after you've got yourself totally situated on the bike should you begin your descent. I rarely kick start my bike . . . instead, I bump start it on my way down."

Chapter 12

PASSING
Tricks of the Trade

Even if you get the hole shot, odds are you'll have to pass slower traffic at some point in the race. It's a difficult challenge at times, but not impossible.

The key is taking different lines than the rider in front of you. That way, if he bobbles, you can slip by fairly easily. Another important aspect of passing is to use your head. Thinking about the pass a little bit can save you a lot of trouble.

Where to Pass

A pass can take place anywhere on the track, but in some places, passing is easier. The most common is in corners, typically on the inside. By squaring off or simply taking a tighter line than the rider in front of you, you'll be set up for a straight drive to the next corner.

Danny Carlson says, "One of the best ways to pass is to outbrake the competition and take their line away."

Done cleanly, you'll get a better drive out of the corner and end up in front, as James Dobb describes: "One of the most common methods is to pass a rider on the inside of the turn. Go underneath the other rider and then outaccelerate them out of the turn. If they have a faster drive on the outside, all you have to do is drift into their line, so they have to back out of the throttle."

Block Passing

Sometimes you need to take the rider's line away to make the pass. This can be part of the end of the pass, when you're exiting the turn, or it can be a bit more deliberate. Taking the rider's line away is known as block passing.

To do this, you have to be inside the rider and turn so you end up interfering with his line. He'll be forced to back off the throttle, and you can motor out front. Done correctly, you'll give him enough room to see what you're doing and ample time to back off. Done incorrectly, you'll cut him off so hard he can't stop, and you'll both end up crashing.

Stuffing

Block passing aggressively is known as stuffing. There's a fine line between block passing and stuffing a rider. You'll see riders stuffing each other to the point where they hit the other guy or even push him off the track. On tight tracks or other special cases, stuffing may be your only option, as Steve Lamson attests: "Depending on the track you're on, sometimes you may have to stuff a rider, especially if the rider is going about the same speed as you. You have to be on the inside of the other guy and a little bit ahead of them, so you can have less risk of falling and taking the other guy out too."

Consult with a friend or your mechanic, as Casey Johnson is doing here, to see if he has any ideas on good places to pass or ways to make up time. An observant eye on the sidelines can catch all kinds of helpful details you can use in a race.

Avoid following riders in the same line, because you increase your chance of falling if they crash. It's also impossible to pass if you're in the same line all the time.

Passing on the Outside

Although the inside line is favored for passing, the outside can also be a good choice. The key here is raw speed. Mike Healey explains, "There are a lot of times where the fastest line will be around the outside of a turn, but people will take the inside so they don't get stuffed. If it looks like the other rider is committing to the inside, then you may want to try the outside and try to slingshot around them."

You can also use an outside line to set up an inside drive. By coming in hard and wide, squaring the corner off deep, and coming back out with a good drive, you can make a solid pass. Danny Carlson favors this method on tight tracks, but with a note of caution: "When there aren't a lot of lines available in the turns, I've found that going to the extreme outside of the corner and then cutting hard to the inside usually allows me to get a good drive to pass riders that are slower than me. The downside is that it uses a lot of energy."

Getting By on the Straights

Sometimes horsepower or a better drive can make the difference. If you can take a rider on a straight, the risk is minimal and the pass will be clean. Jeremy McGrath feels this is one of the simplest ways to pass, and it's a good way to pass lappers with minimal risk. "One of the easiest ways is to outaccelerate the other rider down a straightaway," McGrath says.

Passing in Whoops

Whoops are also good places to pass. If you can find a good alternate line in the whoops, you can often charge by a rider in front of you. Whoops are places where riders make mistakes, so be sure to take a different line than the rider in front of you. If he bobbles, you can pass easily.

Passing off Jumps

Jumps can be used to pass riders, especially if you have a fast line through a particular section. The tough thing about passing on jumps is that you can't change direction much once you're in the air. If you try to pass on a jump, choose an alternative line that gives the rider in front of you plenty of room. Larry Ward recommends, "Try different jump combinations to see if you can find anything that will give you the advantage, even for a second. Once you're ahead, return to the normal race line."

Passing in Corners

1. The most common place to pass is in a corner. This sequence shows two riders—Mike Brown (No. 26) and Damon Huffman (No. 12)—using different lines and coming out in nearly the same place. The classic pass move is to cut to the inside, as Huffman is doing. The other school of thought is to go wide and carry more speed through the corner, as Brown demonstrates.

2. At this point, both riders are side by side. Brown gets a good drive off the previous corner and is carrying more speed, but Huffman's inside line is shorter and requires less speed.

3. It appears the outside line is fastest, because Mike Brown finds a rut and is able to get on the throttle harder. Off-camber turns are difficult, because neither acceleration nor braking can be applied aggressively without the risk of losing traction instantly. Off-camber turns require finesse and excellent throttle and clutch control.

4. Remarkably, both riders are still dead even. Brown needs to corner smoothly and carry quite a bit of speed to make the pass, while Huffman has to square off the corner perfectly and get on the gas as soon as possible. Whoever comes out on top, the rider in front is aware of the pressure. Making a pass stick may require several such attempts. Just keeping the pressure on the rider in front of you can cause him to bobble, leaving the door wide open for you to pass.

PASSING

- Avoid following riders in the same line.
- Look for places to pass during practice.
- Don't try to pass a rider who's riding off his head. Wait for him to make a mistake or crash, then seize the opportunity.
- Outaccelerate the other rider.
- Outbrake the other rider.
- Off-road riders can pass riders through faster pit stops.

When it comes right down to it, anyplace on the track can be good for passing. Stay out of the rider's line and be alert, and the pass may be handed to you on a platter. Steve Lamson favors opportunistic passing and recommends being patient and alert: "I think you have to pass them when you can, but sometimes you have to be patient, because you can do something stupid and make mistakes. It's really bad to follow someone too long, so you need to take advantage of any opportunity that comes up."

Preparation

Passing actually begins early in the day for closed-course riders. Walk the course and look for several good lines in corners, keeping passes in mind. Look for wide spots in the track, especially corners, and consider your strengths as a rider. If you're good in the whoops, spend plenty of time assessing alternative lines through the whoops. If you're good at squaring corners, look for sharp corners with an inside line you can use to dive under other riders. By the time you finish the walk, you should have three or four good places to pass in mind, with a bunch of other possibilities.

In practice, apply the same concepts. Try the lines you found in your walk, as well as

5. As the pair enters the turn, it could go either way. Damon Huffman, who has the inside, could take away Brown's line if he beats him into the turn, and vice versa. Even though you don't get to see the result, it demonstrates one of the fundamental rules of racing—when possible, don't follow the guy ahead of you. Passing is impossible when you're sharing the same line—and if the guy ahead of you falls, you risk getting taken out.

others, and adjust your plans accordingly. Riders are typically going more slowly, so you can probably even practice passing in the spots you've picked out. By the time the gate drops, you'll have some ideas ready on where and how you're going to get around slower riders.

For riders who don't, or aren't allowed, to know the course, where to pass will be determined by opportunity. In those cases, you have to be more creative and opportunistic. Guy Cooper recommends drag racing the guy. "Any time you get in a clear section of the course, try to outaccelerate the other guy, and then beat him to the next obstacle."

Passing with Pit Stops

Long races with pit stops can give you another opportunity to make a pass. "If the course is too tight and the rider you're trying to pass is running almost your same pace, you may be able to pass them in the pits by getting in and out faster. This way, you don't have to worry about making contact and risk crashing," Scott Summers says.

Think!

When making a pass, your brain can be your best friend. Before you go off half-cocked, stuff the guy, and end up off the track, think things through. First off, how much time do you have to make the pass? If you're a fast rider charging up from a bad start in a short moto, you need to pass quickly and take some chances you otherwise wouldn't. Don't be stupid about it (crashing will just send you back

farther), but don't spend a lot of time stalking a rider.

On the other hand, if you're in a two-hour-long hare scramble and are passing a rider who's just a bit slower than you are, it pays to stalk him a while and wait for a good opportunity. Mike Craig prefers this technique for riders who tend to ride over their heads. "If you're trying to pass a guy who's kind of wild, then just wait for them to make a mistake if you can't normally pass them. Watch out, though. Don't wait too long, because you may waste too much time and allow other guys to catch you."

Applying Pressure

A good way to set up a pass is to show the rider a wheel, meaning you pull up close

PASSING

Steve Hatch—"When you walk the track, look for alternative lines that you can use for passing. Know what spots are good ahead of time, so that you can set up the other rider."

Ty Davis—"Rev your bike and yell at the guy to get out of your way. It won't always work, but sometimes they'll move over, or you'll make them nervous enough that they will make a mistake."

Danny Hamel—"Don't try to make a pass unless you're really sure that you're not going to crash. If you go down, you'll waste a lot of time and may even get passed by other riders."

Ken Faught—"Pay close attention to bike setup, so you go to the races with a positive attitude. You don't want any mechanical problems weighing on your mind. Also, make sure you have all your gear ready. Make sure you have a good drink system, comfortable gloves, and tear-offs or Roll-Offs on your goggles."

Dick Burleson—"Work hard to get a really good start. It makes it much easier to race if you don't have to worry about fighting with a bunch of slower riders. When you follow guys that aren't as fast as you, it can affect your mental outlook and allow your competition to break away."

Larry Roeseler—"Make sure you plan your pit stop well, if the race requires one. Time lost in the pits basically means you have to ride faster and take bigger chances to get back on time."

enough so he can see your front wheel. You may not be able to complete the pass, but the rider will know you're pressuring. This can sometimes cause the rider to tighten and make a mistake, leaving the door open for a pass.

In some cases, you can intimidate the rider into making a mistake, as Ron Lechien attests. "One of the oldest tricks is to scare the rider into making a mistake when they're braking. Pull up as close to the rider as you can, grab the clutch, and then rev the bike really high, so it startles the other rider. It even works better if you start yelling at the rider, too. You want to fool them into thinking you're out of control and are going to run into them. They'll usually panic and move over."

Attack, Attack, PASS

If the rider doesn't make a mistake, you have to determine a place to make a pass. If you're on a motocross track, you should already have some ideas of where to pass. This is when you need to follow the rider and watch for your opportunity. "Always stay alert and look for any type of line that could help you make a pass. Every rider has their strengths and weaknesses, and their weakness may be your strength," Danny Hamel says.

Be aggressive, but do your best to avoid contact or taking the other rider out. The issue is not really sportsmanship or any other higher moral ground, but practicality. If you have to collide with the other rider to pass, you can easily end up on the ground, which is the shortest route to the back of the pack.

In most cases, you'll have to show the rider a wheel several times before you can make the pass stick. As you follow the rider, watch his lines and try to figure out when and where there's room for a pass. "Look for alternative lines, maybe places that are the other rider's weak points. That's always the best point for me to pass," says Steve Lamson.

Lamson also favors S-curves to set riders up and knock them off. "Take advantage of S-turns, because they're a good place to set up other riders. You can square the first part

of the turn and then be set up for the next turn and make your pass."

In most cases, a pass is a series of well-calculated moves. Show the rider in front of you a wheel, follow until you have a good idea of some places you can pass, then attack. You may have to set the rider up by simply getting inside or side-by-side through one corner and finishing off the pass in the next. In some cases, it may take a series of three or four corners to finish off the pass.

"Sometimes you'll have to set up for a pass a couple turns ahead. . . . This is where knowing the racetrack pays off. Sometimes there's a good line out of a corner, but it's difficult to get to at your normal speed. Well, when you're being slowed down by another rider, you may be able to use that line," says Ron Lechien.

If you find yourself spending every race passing people, you may have a different problem, as Danny Carlson explains: "If you constantly find yourself behind slower riders, it may be telling you something: you need to work on your starts!"

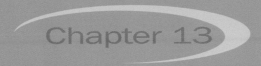

Chapter 13

STARTS
What to Do When the Gate Drops

Many riders will tell you that the start is the single most important aspect of any race. The reasons should be obvious. Riders at the front of the pack can concentrate on riding their own lines, while those at the back have to contend with many factors, such as roost, mud, dust, and slower traffic. Fast lines are hard to come by when you're stuck in the back, and you expend more energy when you're forced to use those harder-to-get-to alternative lines.

Gate Selection

Most of the time, the preferred starting spots are in the middle. You want the shortest, straightest shot to the first turn. Riders starting on the inside or outside get penalized more if they don't get a good drive into the first turn. They may find themselves pinched off in the corner and then passed up by the rest of the field.

On certain starting lines, the outside or inside may be good lines, although they're typically riskier. An outside line can work if you can carry a lot of speed through the corner and come around the pack to the front. The disadvantage is that you could easily find someone in your line and have to brake and lose all your speed, putting you mid-pack at best.

An inside line can work if you can dive under the pack and square the turn. Here again, you can easily get caught in a pileup or simply be slowed down by other riders also diving to the inside.

A good start begins with gate selection and prep. Take this procedure seriously and get to the staging area ahead of your competition. Factory riders have mechanics to do the dirty work, but either way, the job needs to get done.

The key to determining a good line is to watch the gate several races before your moto and see what gate positions seem to produce the most hole shots. More likely than not, you'll find that a bit to the inside or outside of center produces the best results. Have several gate positions in mind, in case you draw poorly and all the spots you planned to use are filled.

Start Procedure

While you're in staging, pay close attention to the start procedure. Watch the starter(s) and look for anything that could help you get a better idea of when they intend to drop the gate. At some tracks, they let the gate fall at the same time every race, while other tracks mix it up a little, so riders can't time the gate and get a premature jump.

Repeated practice is the best way to improve starts. Even if you feel confident, always take a few test starts during practice, to see how well your bike hooks up. You'd hate to start last in a race with this many riders. *Massimo Melani*

A broom is an essential tool for gate prep on concrete starts. At most tracks, you have to supply your own.

Gate Prep

Once you've chosen the gate, prep it. First off, look at your intended route to the first turn and decide the angle of your bike. In most cases, it will be perpendicular to the starting gate, but at some tracks, it may be necessary to angle it slightly. Regardless of the angle, make sure your starting surface is smooth and doesn't have any holes. If the gate is higher than your starting pad, take a shovel and try to raise the level of the dirt. If you start in a hole, your bike will wheelie much more easily and will have to work a lot harder to accelerate. Some tracks allow you to prep your line in front of the starting gate. If so, brush the top layer of soil off with the side of your foot, so you can get to the harder stuff that provides better traction. Toss aside any rocks, mud clods, or other debris that could disrupt your drive.

Mental Preparation

On the starting grid, many riders try to visualize the perfect start in their heads. The key with any good start is total concentration and lightning-quick reflexes.

Gear Selection

Many riders find that first is too low and prefer second. The best way to determine what works for your bike is to practice starts before you get to the race.

Throttle Control

Getting the rear tire hooked up is key to jumping out to the lead. To do that, you need good throttle control. In general, use no more than half throttle until you clear the gate, then roll the throttle open. Also, watch out that you don't start overrevving the bike. Riders tend to raise rpm without knowing it as they wait for the gate to drop. If you rev the bike up and dump the clutch, you'll get too much wheelspin and will be left behind.

Keep conditions in mind as well. On moist, loamy soil, you'll get good traction and

This photo shows the starting pin that holds the gate up. Movement of the pin is the first indication that the gate is dropping.

On the starting grid, take a good, long look at the line you intend to follow to the first turn. Watch for large rocks, mud holes, or other things that could foul up your drive.

can use more throttle on your launch. On concrete pads, traction will be hard to find, and you'll have to use less throttle until the tire clears the pad and bites into the ground.

When you watch the starts before your race, keep an eye on how riders' tires are hooking up. This can give you some clues on how much traction is available.

Clutch Engagement

To speed up your reaction time, find the sweet spot on the clutch. This is the point where the clutch is pulled in just enough to keep the bike from moving. Then, once the gate drops, feed the clutch out slowly to avoid rear wheelspin. If the bike wheelies, use the

Mike Brown, the 2001 AMA 125cc National Motocross Champion, usually arrives at the gate early and tries to visualize the perfect start in his head.

One of the most important tips on concrete starting pads is to heat up the rear tire 15–30 seconds before the gate drops. The idea is to let it spin for a few seconds, so it will become sticky and help you launch out the gate. Don't do it too long, or you'll wear down the knobs—there's a point of diminishing returns.

On concrete surfaces, most riders overrev their bikes and get too much wheelspin once the gate drops. They become impatient and forget about things like clutch control and throttle positioning.

Most riders start with both feet on the ground. This helps maintain balance and keeps the bike pointed in the right direction. The most effective starting technique requires a perfectly straight line, and excessive body language is usually unwanted. Once the gate drops, it's important to get both feet on the pegs as soon as possible, which usually happens within 10–20 feet.

Only 10 feet out of the gate, and you can already see who's in trouble and who has a good chance to pull a hole shot. Most riders' goal is to stretch their initial gear choice until their elbows and shoulders are ahead of the flanking riders. If you throw a shift too early and are the one with your shoulders caught behind, you'll generally lose the drag race to the first turn.

Fifty feet out of the gate, riders have already been pinched out of the main pack, and some are more than a bike length behind. This illustrates the importance of a good launch. Even if the bikes in the back were faster, they don't have any space to pass until they get to the first turn.

Opposite: Keep traction at the rear wheel at all times. On uphill starts, keep your weight centered on the bike or more toward the front, but for the rest of the time, keep your weight on the back of the machine. This allows the front wheel to be light and glide over uneven terrain while the rear wheel puts power to the ground.

Longer starting straights thin the field, until just a few riders battle for the hole shot. Think about braking points, line choices, and any actions you should take, both offensive and defensive.

You can't afford to make a mistake when you're racing at 50 miles per hour this close. The key is to stay focused and look ahead. If you're a few feet behind the leaders, disaster can occur in a split second.

Hole-shot devices made their debut in 2002 and are popular on dirt starts. Here, Larry Ward is compressing his suspension about 4 inches to lock the device into place before he practices a start. The hole-shot unit is spring loaded and pressure sensitive, so it keeps the front end compressed until a rider hits a modest bump or hits the brakes hard. Then the suspension returns to normal.

Four-Stroke Dead-Engine Starts with Scott Summers

By Lee Klancher

Off-road racer Scott Summers has perhaps more experience with four-stroke dead-engine starts than any pro on the circuit. He has five GNCC titles to his credit, with 69 victories in major off-road competitions and a total of nine titles in his trophy case. Summers is infamous for his ability to win on an XR600 four-stroke at a time when the bike was a bit big and not the easiest bike to ride.

After retiring from GNCC competition in 2001 due to injury, Summers came back on the GNCC circuit for 2003 on a CRF450. For perhaps the first time in his career, Summers will be on equipment that is equally matched to his competitors.

Getting good dead-engine starts with a four-stroke is challenging, as Scott readily admits. Perhaps no one on the circuit has as many four-stroke off-road starts as Summers, and he offers up his tips to launching your thumper.

First, be sure the bike is warmed up. This is crucial with four-strokes, which should be warm but not too hot. Do a test start and be sure the bike will fire without the hot start button depressed. Also, Summers says that adjusting the clutch free play so that the clutch fully disengages is key.

1. "Once your engine is good and warm, you want to be sure that you are in gear and that the clutch is fully disengaged. I like to rock the bike back and forth a couple of times to free up the clutch plates so you get a good, clean kick." *Lee Klancher*

2. "Gently turn the engine over until you come to top dead center—the hard spot. On the Honda CRF, I leave the lever just at TDC. Get your leg up and be ready for the starter. I like to wrap all four fingers on the clutch lever so that it is pulled all the way in, rather than using only two fingers as I usually do." *Lee Klancher*

3. "When the starter gun fires, give a solid kick and be careful not to twist the throttle as you kick. Once the engine fires be sure and wait just a second so that it catches and revs before you drop the clutch. If you go too soon, you'll kill it and be kicking as the pack rides away." *Lee Klancher*

4. "Once you are under power, the disadvantage of starting a four-stroke turns into the advantage of four-stroke power. You can hook up better than your two-stroke competitors and, if you are on a CRF, you have a horsepower advantage. Make the most of it by carefully shifting your weight and staying on the gas!" *Lee Klancher*

STARTS

- Get to the gate early for best selection.
- Visualize your entire start, including line choice and braking into the first turn.
- Get familiar with the start procedure before your race.
- Prep your gate for a smooth launch.
- Stay focused.
- Maintain steady throttle control; avoid overrev.
- Minimize wheelspin.
- Use the front brake to avoid rolling into the gate.
- Pay attention to clutch engagement.
- Select the proper gear.
- Lean forward.
- Watch the mechanism.
- Pay careful attention to upshifting.

clutch to drop the front end; otherwise, use it only for shifting until you get to the first corner.

To make sure you don't roll into the gate as you find the sweet spot on the clutch, pull in the front brake with your index finger and then let go of it the moment the gate drops.

Body Position

Lean as far forward as possible. Ideally, both feet should be on the ground, back arched slightly, head over the handlebar, elbows up, and eyes focused on the starting pin. The idea is to hold that position until you make a shift.

Once you're out of the gate, lean your upper body back to increase rear wheel traction and let the tire slip a bit or bring down a wheelie.

STARTS

Greg Albertyn—"Try to stay calm. My best starts always come when I'm most relaxed."

James Stewart—"Practice, practice, and then practice some more. Even when you think you have mastered starts, you still need to practice every time you ride. Getting out of the gate first is one of the keys to winning races."

Steve Lamson—"Concrete starting pads require totally different prep than normal dirt starting gates. On concrete, the idea is to heat up your tire before the start of the race, just like drag racers do. This will help you get really good traction. To do this right, I always have my mechanic clean the concrete with a broom, so I can get more traction. Then, about 15–20 seconds before the gate's supposed to drop, I put my bike in gear, grab onto the front brake, stand on the tips of my toes (to unload the bike), and then spin the rear tire to get it hot and sticky. After that, I focus on the pin and get ready to start, just like normal."

Chad Reed—"I don't think people spend enough time practicing their starts. When you're racing against guys who are your same speed, the only way you are going to beat them is to get a better start or to be in better shape."

Ken Faught—"I always get to the starting line early, so I can watch the timing between the person who's the starter and the person who actually presses the mechanism that drops the gate. I also like to look to line choice into the first turn and for anything else that might give me an advantage."

Ron Lechien—"Way before you go to the line, you have to have some sort of a plan. It starts with getting the best spot on the gate as possible and then leads through to the end of the moto. When I know I'm racing against a lot of fast guys, then it's important to get a good start and get to the front of the pack as soon as possible. When there aren't a lot of fast guys, then you can take your time and ride at your own pace."

Danny Carlson—"Pay attention to where the other riders are on the starting gate, so that you know what to expect. If you know enough history about the riders you're racing against, then you'll know who may come underneath you in the first turn and try to take you out and which riders may be intimidated by you."

Guy Cooper—"Regardless of what type of race you're racing, you want to get the best start possible. This will help you concentrate on riding faster rather than thinking about having to make up for lost time."

Steve Lamson—"Don't let other riders psych you out. Mental games play a part in every race, but try not to get caught up in them. If there is some psyching going on, you'd better be the one doing it."

Watch the Mechanism

Most tracks use backward-falling starting gates that penalize a rider who tries to get an early start. The gate essentially traps the front wheel, forcing you to pull the bike out of its grasp before rejoining the pack. Most gates operate off a cam-type mechanism and have a pin that holds the gate up. Movement of the pin is the first indication that the gate is dropping. Therefore, 10 seconds before the gate is supposed to fall, watch the pin with total concentration, and execute your start once you see it move.

Shifting

You must concentrate on your shifting while racing down the start straight. One missed shift and the pack will leave you in its roost. When you practice starts, pay close attention to how your bike reacts during gear changes. For maximum power to the ground, shift the bike with the throttle wide open and without using the clutch. Some bikes require that the clutch be pulled in or the throttle chopped momentarily to shift.

Two-Stroke Dead-Engine Starts with Mike Lafferty

By Lee Klancher

The best way to get to the front of a race field is to start there. As Mike Lafferty says, "The fewer guys you have to pass, the easier it is to win."

Lafferty offers his tips on dead-engine starts. Mike rips off perfect launches nearly every time, showing off the advantages of dead-engine starts using a two-stroke. In GNCC and other cross-country racing, the start isn't everything, but it doesn't hurt to start the race out front.

1. "I like to use a starting box under my left foot. I position the front of the box even with my footpeg and keep my foot to the front of the box so I can push off it quickly. I put the bike in gear, the engine at TDC, the throttle closed, and the front brake on." *Lee Klancher*

2. "As soon as the engine fires, I twist the throttle, drop the clutch, and drop to the seat in one smooth motion. I keep the power on through to the first turn." *Lee Klancher*

3. "I like to get on the throttle the minute the engine fires, and keep my body weight forward and elbows up." You can see that Mike is getting an amazingly quick drive—his foot has not completed the stroke with the kickstarter, but the back tire is already digging. *Lee Klancher*

4. "I like to leave the kickstart lever out until after the first turn. I want all my energy and balance focused on the start, and I feel that little bit to knock the lever back shouldn't be used up during the start." *Lee Klancher*

Profile of a Perfect Start

1. Three-time AMA 125cc National Motocross Champion Ricky Carmichael is one of the best starters of all time. He usually arrives at the gate very early and then tries to visualize the perfect start in his head.

2. Even though Carmichael's mechanic has already cleaned the concrete launch pad, he repeats the process to wipe away dirt that fell down once the bike was rolled into position.

3. This sequence clearly shows how important traction is to a good start. On concrete surfaces, most riders tend to overrev their bikes and get too much wheelspin once the gate drops. Generally, the tendency is to get impatient and forget about things like clutch control and throttle positioning.

4. Notice that Carmichael starts with both feet on the ground. This is something that helps him keep his balance out of the blocks. The most effective starting technique requires a perfectly straight line, and excessive body language is usually unwanted.

5. You can already see that Carmichael has a distinct advantage even though this trio has only traveled 2 feet. The goal of most riders is to stretch their initial gear choice until their elbows and shoulders are ahead of the flanking riders. If you throw a shift too early and you are the one with your shoulders caught behind, you'll generally lose the drag race to the first turn.

6. This photo shows how wheelspin has negatively affected Casey Johnson's (No. 16) start. You can see the tread pattern on Carmichael's and Stephane Roncada's (No. 22) rear tires, but Johnson's is just a blur. Johnson has also shifted his body weight to the right and is trying to compensate for the loss of traction. Wheelspin will also cause a bike to slide sideways off of the launching pad.

7. Carmichael has slowly returned his left foot to the peg by drawing it straight up. He's ready to make his first shift and has already started to increase engine rpm.

8. Carmichael has done everything right and is already a full foot ahead of the other riders in this picture. RC was rewarded with yet another hole shot.

Gary Semics on Starts

"What I do is prepare myself until I know I can do what I have to do."
— Joe Namath

All the other techniques apply to starts, but here are some especially for starts. There are two races in each moto—from the starting gate around the first turn and from the first turn to the checkered flag. If you lose the race to the first turn, you're going to have to work that much harder to win the second race.

Starting Technique

1. This sequence follows one of Craig Anderson's (No. 109) starts. He gets out of the gate well and leads the pack of riders into the first turn. He's diving to the inside line to make the shortest path from point A to point B.

SIT UP FRONT

Sit on the front part of the seat, with your head over the handlebar clamps.

It's pretty obvious you need to sit on the front part of the seat to pull a good hole shot, but I've seen riders sitting on the middle of the seat and not even know it.

This makes it impossible to get your weight far enough forward to keep the front end down when you have good traction.

When you sit on the front of the seat, your weight is at the center of the motorcycle, right over the motorcycle's pivot point. As you launch off the line and down the front straight, stay at the front of the seat and transfer

weight by leaning forward or back.

When it comes to starts, start off on the front part of the seat and stay there until you exit the first turn.

MOVE FORWARD FOR TRACTION

Lean your upper body backward to increase rear wheel traction,

2. Once he gets into the turn, he goes from standing to sitting and sticks out his inside leg for balance. If he bobbles, he has the option to dab the leg if he thinks it might keep him upright. Sitting down in this first turn is possible only because the turn is fairly smooth. Had it been rough, Anderson might have stood the entire way around.

3. Anderson's line choice makes him the clear leader as they apex the first turn. He has to be extremely careful, because a wrong move could mean he gets run into from behind and run over by the pack of riders.

4. The first turn is the busiest place on any racetrack. You have to be alert at all times, and you have to pick your lines carefully. Usually the people on the outside have the greatest risk of crashing, because overaggressive riders may try to outbrake them and overshoot the first turn.

and lean forward to keep the front wheel down.

When a nervous novice starts, he usually leans forward and freezes there, no matter what traction conditions are like. Be aware of what kind of traction you're going to get. This way, you'll know how much you should lean forward, stay in the middle, or even lean back if it's real slippery (like on a smooth cement start). Adjust your weight according to traction.

TWO FEET DOWN

Start with both feet down in front of the footpegs until you need to shift. Put your feet back on the footpegs when you need to upshift.

Riders make a lot of mistakes on starts. Here are some of the most common ones:

Starting off with your feet to the outside of the footpegs. (They can easily move back under acceleration.)

Starting off with your feet in back of the footpegs. (They'll end up behind you.) When your feet go behind the pegs, the result is poor balance, too much weight behind the pivot point, and an inability to shift to the next gear on time.

Trying to put your feet back

on the footpegs as soon as you start to move. (You aren't maintaining good balance.)

If you keep your feet down in front of the footpegs, they'll stay there throughout your start. This gives you better balance, keeps your overall body weight more forward, and leaves you in a good position to shift to the next gear when you need to.

When you want to shift, pull your left leg up and hit the shifter with the top of your boot as you put your foot back on the footpeg. It may take a little practice, but once you get it down, it's the best way to go out of the gate.

5. Anderson drifts wide and runs away with the lead. Drifting wide allows him to maintain momentum, which is key in this type of drag race situation.

RELEASE THE CLUTCH SMOOTHLY

Feed the power to the rear wheel with the clutch and throttle as quickly and smoothly as possible.

The most common mistake here is to dump the clutch too quickly or slip it too long. To get a good start, it's necessary to be quick, but at the same time you have to be smooth and precise with your clutch control. About the only place you can just dump the clutch and gas it is in deep sand. Otherwise, you have to feed the power to the rear wheel with the clutch and throttle together. This means you have to open the throttle and let the clutch out according to traction.

Be like a gunfighter on the start: relaxed, smooth, and lightning fast.

MOVE THAT BODY

Move your upper body from side to side to compensate and keep the motorcycle straight out of the gate.

Some riders freeze into one body position when they come out of the gate and just stay in that position. Or they drop their elbows and twist their upper bodies, to try to keep the motorcycle from veering over out of the gate. They don't have total control, because they fail to move correctly as things change.

An important movement to maintain this control out of the gate is side-to-side upper body movement. Start off with a lot of overgrip, so your elbows can remain fairly high. From this position, you can move your shoulders parallel back and forth across the handlebars, to keep the motorcycle straight out of the gate. To get used to the proper movement, practice this in a stationary position.

Chapter 14

PRACTICE
The Only Road to the Top

The most important part of riding technique is good body position, and the only way to develop better body position is to practice. The importance of these two facets of riding cannot be overstated.

Professional riders get to the level they are by hours and hours of practice. Talent, conditioning, and desire are all a part of excelling in off-road riding, but these three things are not enough. You have to practice.

Practice doesn't have to be grueling and repetitive, especially for amateur riders (most of us). Go out and try different things. Trail ride and explore side trails, climb banks and hills, or practice broadsliding down fire roads. Even within a small riding area, there are always new challenges. Experimenting is one of the most entertaining things to do with your bike and one of the best ways to learn.

Learning body position isn't always fun, and the position isn't always natural. The key is practicing the correct position until it becomes natural. Once you have that, everything else comes more easily.

Improving your riding skills is not always an easy task. The learning curve is steep for beginning riders, and it gets tougher with time. Regardless of your current ability, however, you can take several steps to improve. Keep in mind that the only way you're going to improve is through practice.

Take the time to set up your bike properly. The world is full of suspension companies who can help you get your bike dialed in if you don't feel confident doing it yourself. If it isn't set up correctly, you'll never be able to reach your full potential, and you risk personal safety. Guy Cooper demonstrates setting sag in his garage. To properly set race sag, his feet shouldn't touch the ground.

Static Drills

A basic place to start learning new skills is with the bike on the stand. Climb aboard and put yourself in the proper body position. Go step by step, making sure your elbows and head are up, you're overgripping the throttle, your feet are centered on the pegs, you have one finger on the clutch and brake levers, and your head is over the handlebar mount.

The single most important ingredient to improved skill is practice. The more time you spend in the saddle, the more comfortable you'll become. Here, Dick Burleson rides in Texas, where he has miles and miles of trails and tracks to practice on. _Karel Kramer_

To become well rounded, try to ride in as many types of terrain as possible—don't limit your riding to one track or riding area. This is one of the most important aspects of improving, and it will give you more confidence.

Once you're in the proper position, practice sitting, standing, and shifting your weight forward and back in both positions. Pay close attention to where your body is when you move. You'll probably slip out of position once in a while and can correct it. This whole drill takes only a few minutes, and if you do it regularly, it can really help you improve body position. You can do it on a rainy day, after you adjust the chain, or just when you've got the itch to ride but can't get out to do so.

Challenging Terrain

When it comes to riding, one of the best ways to practice is to try different types of terrain. Try a new riding area. Go trail riding for the day. A day spent jumping logs, crossing streams, and tackling gnarly hills is a great way for a motocross rider to improve, and a day at the track can be a great outing for an enduro rider. The broader your horizons, the more comfortable and skilled you'll become.

Try a little trials-style riding. Ride along at a walking pace and hop over logs, big rocks, or short embankments. Keep your body in the proper position, and use the engine's low-end power and controlled bursts to tackle obstacles. This is both a good practice technique and a good way to warm up. (Hopping on your bike and immediately reeling off fast laps is a good way to pull muscles and increase the likelihood of injury; a few minutes of warmup will save you a lot of pain.)

Wheelies and Stoppies

Wheelies and stoppies are also good practice techniques. Slow wheelies, where you use balance and engine torque to ride a walking-pace wheelie, are especially good for learning throttle control, balance, and body position. Keep your foot on the rear brake, and hit it if you start to loop out.

Stoppies are done by sitting in a normal or slightly forward body position and braking hard enough to raise the rear wheel off the ground. Start small, at low speeds, with gradual brake applications. Keep your elbows bent and your body loose and relaxed. If the rear end comes up too high, simply release the front brake.

As a variation, place your weight back and practice locking up the front wheel rather than doing a stoppie. Again, start practicing at a walking pace and work up to higher speeds. These slow practice techniques are a good way to become familiar with how your bike reacts to different situations. They're also a great way to just goof around and have fun on your bike.

Pounding out Laps

Motocross riders should spend some time just pounding out laps. Pick a set number of laps and run those as hard as you can. This can be a good time to focus on a particular technique, especially the basics. Late in the moto is when your technique is most likely to sag, so concentrate on keeping your body in the right position as you get tired.

Don't mindlessly pound out laps. Pick a technique of the day and work on it for a bunch of laps. Spend one day working on nothing but keeping your outside elbow high in corners. On another day, concentrate on braking technique. On another, work on using the clutch to get a smooth drive. You'll want to cut some laps just letting it all hang out, putting all your skills together, but you need to focus on specific techniques to improve.

Outside Help

Have a buddy watch you ride and critique your riding. Explain to him what you should be doing. Better yet, show him photos from the book that demonstrate proper riding technique. Then have him watch you ride and give you some feedback. Are your elbows high? Is your head up? Are you staying forward on the bike?

Videotape is also an extremely useful tool. As they say, seeing is believing. No matter what level your riding skills, you'll see something and will want to change it. You may be shocked to find you're doing things exactly the opposite of the way you thought.

Riding Schools

One of the best ways to improve your riding is to attend a riding school. You'll find a number of them in the resource list at the end of the book. All these folks can give you valuable feedback on your riding, along with tips and techniques that will make you a faster, smoother rider. Plus, riding school can be a good time.

If you race motocross, spend a portion of each riding session pounding laps. Practice for a set amount of time, such as 10, 15, 20, or 30 minutes, to simulate racing. When possible, ask a friend to check your lap times, and keep track of them in a notebook. If they get progressively slower, chances are you need to work on your conditioning.

Have Fun

No matter where you ride, do some play riding. This sport is fun, remember? Ride a wheelie. Try setting up for a corner in the air. Do some long power slides. Stay loose and have a good time. Anything you do on the bike that's fun is good practice.

Take your time. This applies to both practice and racing. Many riders press just a little too hard and go slower because of it. If you slow down just a bit, you'll be able to see the track better and will find yourself speeding up. Practice is the best time to do this.

Watch faster riders. What are they doing differently? What lines are they taking? Watch the pros on television or at a race and check out what the local riders are doing. If you get a chance to ride with faster riders, don't pass it up. Follow them and learn (but be careful not to get sucked into trying something above your ability).

All these techniques aside, the single most important thing is simply to ride as much as you can. The more you ride, the better you'll be. If you spend some of your riding time concentrating on improving, you'll get better more rapidly, but riding itself makes you a better rider. It's that simple.

Watch race coverage on television, to see how professional racers tackle various race courses. Look at their race lines, passing techniques, and other strong points. Many professional athletes, such as baseball, football, and hockey players, study films extensively to learn more about themselves, their opponents, and the sport in general.

Opposite: Have a friend videotape you in action. This way, you can see for yourself what you're doing right and wrong, and you can watch it over and over. This is one of the best ways to break bad habits, because sometimes you may think you're doing something one way when, in fact, you're doing it totally differently.

Motocross and off-road riders alike should spend a portion of their daily routine play riding. Practice throwing the bike around off jumps, learning how to wheelie, and similar maneuvers. Try some of these moves at slower than normal speeds, to learn better balance, as Danny Carlson is doing here. (You may even consider trials-type riding on your normal machine.) Also, go trail riding every once in a while. Multi-time supercross champ Jeremy McGrath is proof that play riding pays big dividends. "It's the best way to get real familiar with your bike," McGrath says. "It gives you a good feeling how the bike will react if you get sideways or if the front wheel is too high or too low."

Sometimes, the best way to go faster is to actually slow down. Riding too aggressively, many riders work against themselves by making mistakes. The more mistakes you make, the more tired you'll become.

Following faster riders is a good way to figure out faster lines on the track. Pay close attention to their body position, brake markers, acceleration points, engine rpm, and any other items that may help. Be careful, though. This is one way to get sucked into doing something beyond your riding ability.

Practice braking later, but only in areas where you have plenty of runoff room, in case you make a mistake. Braking later is one of the best ways to condition your senses to higher speeds.

Chapter 15

ADAPTING TO DIFFERENT BIKES

How Weight and Horsepower Affect Riding Technique

Sitting side by side, most 125 and 250 two-strokes produced by the same manufacturer appear to mirror one other. They have identical wheels, the same seat height, similar ergonomics, and many more common characteristics.

The two machines are, in fact, radically different because of their power output. The amount and type of horsepower produced is so different that each bike requires a different riding style. Likewise with 80s, open bikes, and four-strokes.

The primary reason is a combination of the power-to-weight ratio and power delivery. Bigger motors build horsepower almost instantaneously, but they also increase overall bike weight. In some cases, engine size can add so much weight that the size becomes a disadvantage. Conversely, the much smaller and lighter-weight 80s and 125s handle incredibly well but suffer in the motor department.

Another factor that affects riding style is technology. It wasn't too long ago that open bikes were fairly popular. Unfortunately, most manufacturers did little chassis, suspension, and engine development during the early to mid-1990s, which has nearly pushed the class into extinction. The lighter and predominantly better-handling 250s produce horsepower levels that rival their much larger kin. Combined with better suspension, it's easy to see why 250s outsell open bikes by a huge margin. Open bikes still suit a certain type of

Most riders enjoy 125s because they handle so well. The chassis is similar to a 250, but most 125s weigh approximately 15 pounds less. This may not seem like a lot, but the decreased weight makes quite a difference. The bikes are easier to flick, and the suspension works much better with the lower weight. The only weakness is that 125s have less horsepower than larger bikes and a narrow powerband. To go fast on a 125, you need to carry more speed than with larger bikes.

It's easy to see why 250s are the most popular two-stroke engine displacement on the planet. In most cases, they offer the best compromise between horsepower and weight. They have plenty of earth-churning, roost-throwing power, and they're fairly nimble.

Riding 80cc machines is similar to riding 125s. The lack of engine displacement requires lots of engine rpm to build horsepower. Fast mini riders have to pay close attention to frequent gear changes, along with constant clutch use and precise throttle control.

rider, but modern 250s are easier to ride for most of us.

Fortunately, technology has been kind to 80s, 125s, and 250s, and environmental issues have forced manufacturers to spend more time and money on four-stroke development. The decline of two-stroke open bikes has been helped along by the advances in 250cc and 450cc four-stroke engines, which have become good enough to win races in every major racing series the world over. In fact, four-strokes now represent the future of off-road motorcycling, and this will soon have an effect on the future development of all two-strokes.

Choosing a Size

One of the best characteristics of engine displacement, or lack thereof, is that it doesn't discriminate. Regardless of engine size, nearly every bike is capable of providing unlimited fun.

There are no strict guidelines to choosing bike size. While it's true that motocross tends to overlook open bikes and four-strokes, bigger engine displacements of 250cc or more are popular for desert riding, hill climbing, and sand dunes, where speed and horsepower are basic necessities.

"There are huge differences in the various engine sizes, and they all require different riding styles," says Mike Healey, who has raced virtually every size of two- and four-stroke motorcycle in National- and/or World Championship–caliber events.

"When I rode 80s, I remember that it was real important to keep the revs up, especially as I got bigger. Minis are pretty dead off bottom, but once they come alive, they can feel as fast as a 125."

"It's real important to pay attention to shifting on 80s," says Danny Carlson. "Most minis are pretty picky and won't work that well when ridden a gear too high or too low."

Most 80s are designed for teenagers, so the engine is packaged in a small chassis. Typically, a 125 is the smallest displacement of a normal-size frame.

"On 125s, you can be more aggressive in the turns than on a 250, mostly because of the weight," says Mike Metzger. "You can hold the throttle on longer and accelerate much

Opposite: Because of their extraordinary power, open bikes are extremely potent and brutally fast. Precise throttle delivery and liberal clutch use are required to keep rear wheelspin to a minimum. The one disadvantage most open bikes have is weight. Generally they're less maneuverable than 125s and 250s, which affects every aspect of riding, and they have a tendency to tire riders easily.

80/125/250/ OPEN AND FOUR-STROKE

- **Make sure you feel comfortable with the size of your motorcycle.**
- **The 80s and 125s require more rpm and clutch work to use effectively.**
- **The 250s have ample power in a broad range, giving you the option of riding with more rpm and clutch work or exiting turns a gear higher.**
- **Open bikes are usually ridden a gear high, to smooth out power and reduce vibration.**
- **Four-strokes usually offer smooth power delivery and require you to maintain momentum, because they don't build revs as explosively as a two-stroke.**

quicker, because they handle better. Aboard 125s, it's usually best to ride with your weight towards the back of the bike. This way, you can keep the front end light and add traction to the rear wheel. Since 125s don't have as much power as the larger bikes, it's really important to maintain constant traction."

For riders moving up from 80s or those who want the best-handling full-size bike, 125s are a good choice. Although 125s can be difficult to ride due to the power delivery, they handle well, are easy to throw around, and are a joy to ride. The 125s aren't as good for off-road and enduro riding, though, and aren't quite as flexible as the larger machines.

The 250s

Moving up in engine size, the 250s are the easiest to ride and have become the premier class in motocross racing. The power-band is broader, with more low end than an 80 or 125. They also have enough power to accelerate out of mistakes. On a smaller bike, if you totally blow a corner, it'll take some time (and clutch abuse) to get that lost momentum back. On a 250, momentum is only a twist of the wrist away. The final benefit is that 250 engines tend to require less maintenance than a smaller bike. Considering all this, it's no surprise 250s are the best-selling two-strokes in the United States.

"Two-fifties offer the best of both worlds," Healey says. "They're much lighter than an open bike, yet they're way more powerful than a 125. I'd say a 250 is the best all-around size."

"I actually find that I have to concentrate more on 250s than on 125s," says Metzger. "Throttle control seems more important—otherwise, you can get in deep trouble pretty fast."

For most riders, 250s are the best choice. Power is ample, and the powerband is broad and relatively easy to use. Motocross bikes usually have power flexible enough for a broad range of riding types and can be modified to work well in any kind of race. Enduro bikes, such as KTM's 250E/XC, can be ideal for more casual riders as well. They're a little easier to ride than motocross bikes and work well for a broad range of conditions. You probably won't win a motocross race on one, but you could certainly race an occasional moto and have a good time. Whichever you choose, the only real drawback is that 250s tend to be more expensive. But because they're the most popular size, more machines are available, at least in the used market.

Open Class Bikes

The larger open bikes require a totally different riding style. Their power delivery used to be smoother than the smaller bikes, but modern open-classers have a pretty awesome hit. They have lots of low-end power on tap and don't require as much shifting. They also require less maintenance than smaller bikes.

"On open bikes, it's important to ride them with your weight centered or slightly towards the front, to keep from wheelying," Healey says. "And because they're much

heavier than the other bikes, you can't throw them around as much. Plus, you have to do your braking earlier, to slow down in time."

"Most of the time, it's better to ride an open bike a gear high. This will smooth out the low-end hit and reduce the amount of shifting. They also won't vibrate as bad," says Ron Lechien. "Truthfully, open bikes usually don't do that well when they're overrevved, unless they have a lot of serious motor work done to them."

Open bikes are the bike of choice for desert racers, where their abundant power is needed to push the bikes through deep sand at high speeds. Big-bores can also work well for vet riders or trail riders. The advantages are an abundance of low-end power and lower maintenance costs. However, these bikes make a ton of horsepower and can get you into trouble quickly. Without thoughtful throttle control, you'll end up on your head.

Thumpers

In the world of four-strokes, the horse-power-to-weight ratio is important, but its effects are reduced for two reasons: in general, four-strokes weigh more than comparably sized two-strokes, and they usually don't produce as much power. Therefore, engine displacement is typically larger, to help compensate for the differences. This is why 250cc four-strokes are allowed to race against 125cc two-strokes and why 450cc four-strokes are classed with 250cc two-strokes in AMA and FIM competition.

The most important difference with four-stroke engines is power delivery. They tend to give you a smooth, extremely broad power-band. Four-strokes don't rev as quickly as two-strokes, but the power is typically more controllable. In conditions where traction is hard to find, such as slippery rocks or slimy off-camber turns, a four-stroke's more progressive power delivery makes it easier to handle, especially for lower-level riders. In deep sand or long straights, a four-stroke will give up some time to the two-stroke engines, which tend to have more top-end power and nearly instantaneous delivery.

Honda XRs are classic examples, with controllable, easy-to-use power. You may not have as much as the guy next to you, but you'll be able to use all of it. However, some high-end four-strokes are built for motocross and have a powerband more like a two-stroke

Four-strokes require a different starting technique than two-strokes. It's not difficult, but it does require a little practice.

engine. Just the same, their advantage is hooking up out of the turns with a more progressive delivery of power.

"One of the coolest things about four-strokes is that they love to be flat-tracked around turns," says Healey, "Especially big sweepers. Use this to your advantage if you're dicing with someone on a two-stroke."

"I usually ride a four-stroke like an open bike, since the two handle real similar," says motocross and off-road champ Ty Davis. "I try to take wide lines whenever possible, to conserve energy and to keep up momentum."

For off-road, trail, or beginning riders, a four-stroke is ideal. Four-strokes are easier to ride and typically require less maintenance than two-strokes. They're becoming more prevalent in the upper echelons of racing as well. Doug Henry won the 1997 Las Vegas supercross on a Yamaha YZ400F, and Kevin Windham used a

Honda CR450R in 2003 to stop Ricky Carmichael's streak of 26 consecutive moto wins in the AMA 250cc National Championship MX Series.

On the off-road side of things, Ty Davis has proven lethal in a Yamaha 450, Shane Watts has won several GNCCs on 400s and 525s, Mike Kiedrowski won the 2001 WORCS (World Off-Road Championship Series) on a Suzuki DR-Z400, and Honda's XR650R rules Baja in the hands of Johnny Campbell. Four-strokes are now competitive in all forms of motocross and off-road.

Ultimately, the decision on bike size and engine style is yours. Take a long, hard look at your riding level and the places you'll ride, and you can figure out which bike makes the most sense for you. A good way to get an idea of what suits you is to look at a wide assortment of bikes. If you look at used machines, you can often arrange to take a test ride. You might

think you want a motocross bike, but you may find in a test ride that the power delivery is too violent and may decide to look for a four-stroke or enduro bike instead.

If motocross racing is your only desire, by all means look at a motocross bike. But motocross bikes are built for one purpose—racing on MX tracks—and are a handful in most conditions, especially for riders just starting out. If you want to try a broad range of riding and are just getting started, take a look at other off-road bikes. Bikes such as Kawasaki KDXs, Yamaha TTRs, the Suzuki DR-Zs, Honda XRs, and KTM E/XCs are a blast to ride and can handle most any kind of terrain. From reading this book, you've probably discovered that a key to going fast is being relaxed and comfortable. That's hard to do when the bike delivers more power than you can use every time you open the throttle!

Chapter 16

STRATEGY
Power of the Mind

There's a lot more to racing than pinning the throttle and trying to ride your fastest. Any racer in any sport will tell you strategy is always involved.

One of the most important aspects of strategy is simply having one. If you go to the gate with a plan, you'll be better prepared for the race. Obviously, a good strategy is better than a lousy one, but a plan is important for you to succeed.

Strategy can be applied on several levels, from passing strategy to a strategy for the season or your career. It can apply to everything from bike setup to setting up a pass. For starters, consider strategy that can be applied to a particular moto or race.

Race Log

A good place to start forming a strategy is with a race log or notebook. This book includes a useful sheet on bike setup you can photocopy. In addition to notes about your bike, make notes about the track and your riding. Is there a section where you were particularly fast? Did you crash? Where and why? Where did you get passed frequently? Note anything else significant. Was it dusty? Muddy? What was the traction like? Once you've ridden a track and written it in your log book, you can review your notes the night before or in the car on the way to the race and start to form your strategy.

Don't get caught up in mind games, because they'll wear on you, both on and off the track. Instead, concentrate on your own race program and how you can be a better rider.

Winning races takes desire, determination, and hard work. Australia's Craig Anderson came to the Southwick 125cc National in 2003 and won the race, even though he'd never seen the track before.

Always have a strategy mapped out before you go to the starting line.

If you don't have notes but have raced the course, take some time to remember what you can about it. If possible, do a mental lap of the course, remembering as much detail as you can. Figure out the sections where you did well and where you did poorly. Think about why you were fast or slow. What could you do differently to go faster? What do you need to continue doing to keep your advantage?

Walk the Track

The next important step is to walk the track. As you go around the track, match your mental picture to what you see. Where have lines changed? Where can you pass? This is also a good time to talk to your race buddies and see what they're doing, especially if they're faster than you.

Consider how the track will change. If it's soft sand, you can expect ruts to form. If you know the track well, make a mental note of where ruts will form and how you can turn that to your advantage.

Visualize the Race

When you get back to the pits, take some time to sit down and imagine a lap. Focus on a simple thing to work on in each corner. If you're really into it, draw a map of the track and make a note at each obstacle.

In practice, try some of these strategies and adjust as necessary. This is an especially good time to try several different lines and get a feel for whether your theories work. Afterward, go back to the pits and sit down again, adjusting your mental picture of the track.

Assembling Race Strategy

At this point, you have a picture of the track and how to attack it. Factor in the race conditions, number of competitors, quality of the competition, and your conditioning to form a strategy for the race. For example, if it's a short race with lots of entrants and your conditioning is suspect, concentrate on getting a good start, charging as hard as you can in the first lap, and conserving energy for the rest of the race.

Let's say you conserve energy by slowing down a fraction in a long whoop section and into some wicked braking bumps, since these two places sap a lot of energy. Use the best line to hold off any passes and concentrate on keeping your speed up on the smoother parts of the track.

You'll probably want some kind of strategy for the start as well. Watch some starts, check out the best lines, and factor in your personal style to come up with a sound strategy off the line.

STRATEGY

Strategy is a key to success. Professionals got to where they are with hard work, talent, and a plan for success. Here's a sampling of some of the strategies used by the world's fastest riders.

Jeremy McGrath—"I always try to get to the front as fast as possible. Then I try to open up a comfortable lead and, depending on how things are going, I know if I can let up or if I need to ride harder. Having a cushion is important, because it means that you don't have to take as many chances in order to win."

Steve Lamson—"No matter what, it's important to never give up. In 1995, I was over 50 points down in the 125 National Championship, and I didn't think winning was really possible. But I decided to give it my all and take each race one at a time. In the end, it came down to the final moto, but I wound up winning. Had I given up at any time, the title would have gone to someone else."

Jeremy McGrath—"I always pay attention to my bike in practice and in each moto, so I can make any necessary changes for my next ride."

Ron Lechien—"Part of the strategy is to find places to pass in practice and then remember them later. I always try every line in practice, so I know what works and what doesn't."

Mike Kicdrowski—"I walk part of the track before each moto, so I can see how the lines have changed. This helps out a lot, especially the first lap of the race."

Danny Carlson—"The night before the race, I try to get really good sleep. I go to bed at the normal time and then get up early enough to take a shower and eat breakfast on the way to the track."

Steve Lamson—"After practice and between motos, I try to get as much rest as possible."

Danny Carlson—"I always go to the bathroom before I go to the line. During a race you can't stop, and I find that I don't ride that well when I'm uncomfortable."

Dick Burleson—"If you are serious about racing, make sure you are serious about physical fitness. Top riders like Ricky Carmichael and James Stewart are as fast at the end of the race as they are at the beginning. This is really important, because the level of competition at the top has never been more intense."

Mike Kiedrowski—"I usually have someone videotape practice, so I can see what myself and the other riders are doing right and wrong. This really helps out a lot."

Scott Summers—"At races where I know there will be a pit stop, I try to have everything organized, so I can get in and get out. I have a plan ahead of time that includes refueling, getting new goggles and gloves if I need them, plus replacing any broken parts. I always have all of my tools laid out in plain view, where they are easy to grab, and I have spare bars and wheels ready to go."

Steve Hatch—"I always want to know as much about the course as I can, so I always try to walk it. I look for anything that can give me an advantage to help me win."

James Stewart—"Never give up. You never know what is going to happen to the other people in front of you. Remember, winners never quit, and quitters are never winners."

Ty Davis—"At enduros, I always pay close attention to my mileage and time. When I come in early, I try to check my bike over to make sure there are no problems."

Scott Summers—"It's a good idea to make sure that your mechanic is really familiar with your bike and understands everything about the type of racing that you're doing. My mechanic, Fred Bramblett, is one of the best, because he thinks like a racer and knows that some races are decided in the pits. There's nothing worse than coming in for fuel and having your pit crew running over each other as they try to get things taken care of."

Larry Roeseler—"In extremely long races, like Baja or Six Days, you have to make sure your equipment lasts—otherwise, you may not be able to finish."

Scot Harden—"In dusty races, you never want to follow people for too long, because it can be dangerous and will ruin your air filter. Dust will only slow you down. That's why I always do whatever is possible to get around a rider who's dusting me out."

When you come to the line, have several strategies in place: a plan of attack for the start, a general plan for the course of the race, and some specific ideas on fast lines and places to pass. This plan of attack will give you a better focus and is likely to get you better results, mainly because some of the questions that will come up have already been answered.

Thinking Long-Term

Strategy also applies on a larger scale to riders competing in a series or making long-term goals with their riding. Your goal may be a National Championship or simply to bring your riding up and compete in your first race. Whatever it is, take a little time to make a plan that will guide you in your goal. In any type of series race, the idea is usually to score as many points as possible at each round, even if it means riding with failing equipment—hence the phrase "every point counts." For the rider planning a first race, some conditioning, a regular riding schedule, and showing up for a practice day or two at the track could be a good strategy.

"Part of any strategy requires finishing," says Bob Hannah. "You have to be mentally strong in any race, and that means knowing your bike can do its job."

Part of any off-road strategy should include pit stops. Have all your tools and spare parts organized and easily accessible, to speed up work time.

Gary Semics on Strategy

"Whether you think you can or think you can't, you are right."

— Henry Ford

Think to win. Conditioning, practice, and training are all important to finding the front of the pack, but your brain is your most powerful weapon on the track.

LOOK AHEAD

Look far enough ahead of you to be ready for what's coming up. If you can't see it (because of an obstacle), remember what's there.

This is one of those things that most riders don't even think about, but it's important, and it's not really a natural thing for most riders. It has to be learned and practiced. The most common mistake is to always look too close in front of you and not look ahead far and soon enough. Don't race the track by every 10 feet. Race it one section at a time and blend the sections together with a purpose. When done correctly, it's an art form. When you go beyond that, it's magic.

You should always be scanning the track in front of you, focusing on the most important thing, then scanning and focusing on the next most important thing, and so on. If you can't see it yet, remember what's there. Ride with this main focus and your peripheral vision. Always be ready for what's coming up well before you get there. Set yourself up so you're going to be on the right line well in advance. And if you're trying to pass someone, look beyond him, not at him.

You can't win races by following people.

Forming a plan is half the battle to success on the track. Here Brian Swink gets some advice.

Chapter 17

FOUR-STROKES
How to Use This Different Motor Type to Your Advantage

The introduction of aggressive four-stroke motorcycles by Yamaha, KTM, Husaberg, and Honda has opened the minds of many riders. No longer are four-strokes viewed as slow, heavy, and dated. They're true competition bikes in every aspect, and in some types of racing they've proven to be a sizable advantage.

In fact, it started years ago, when Doug Henry used a Yamaha YZ400F to win the 1998 AMA 250cc National Motocross Championship, Joel Smets won the 1998 FIM 500cc World Championship, and Scott Summers rode a big-bore Honda XR600R to several AMA Grand National Cross Country Championships. Think again if you believe two-strokes are the only way to go.

While engine design is the biggest distinguishing factor between a four-stroke and its reed-valve relative, the type of power delivery affects every aspect of performance. Braking, suspension, and even starting procedures are influenced by the four-stroke powerplant, mandating a different type of riding style. Sure, they share a lot of traits, but if you know the differences between the two types of engine, you'll be a better rider.

Engine

Depending on the type of four-stroke and whether it has an automatic or manual compression release, something as simple as

Four-strokes don't respond well to deep ruts, but they do appreciate berms, especially those that are really wide.

starting can be a challenge. Typically, four-strokes are more difficult to start than two-strokes, but once you get the procedure figured out, it shouldn't be at all intimidating.

From the moment you let the clutch out, you'll notice that power delivery is different. In general, four-strokes produce less wheelspin and more traction. This is a definite advantage

during acceleration, but how four-strokes build momentum is what makes them unique.

In most cases, four-strokes don't respond well to excessive clutch use. While the clutch can be effective in a lot of instances, it's not nearly as important as on two-strokes. Generally, four-strokes work best when the throttle is applied in a roll-on

While two-stroke bikes favor cut-and-thrust riding styles, four-strokes are better at wide lines. The explosiveness of a two-stroke engine allows the rider to come close to a stop in a corner (as when you square off a corner inside a berm) and accelerate hard enough to maintain or gain time on the rider in the outside line. Four-stroke riders don't have that luxury. Smooth power and a heavier bike mean cut-and-thrust is not the technique of choice. Go wide, roll on the throttle early, and tractor out of the corners.

Racing rules allow 250cc four-stokes to compete in the 125cc class. Four-strokes typically weigh more than comparably sized two-strokes, and they usually don't produce as much power. Engine displacement is usually larger to compensate for the differences. This is Yamaha of Troy's Brock Sellards in action. *Ken Faught*

fashion. These motors produce a lot of torque down low, and the addition of the extra parts, such as cam chain and cam(s), increases spinning mass, which means that "double-clutching it" doesn't build engine rpm as quickly to provide added boost. Hence, consistent throttle application with minimal clutch use is usually way more effective.

Four-strokes are usually a little more sluggish during the beginning of acceleration. The motor makes most of its power in midrange and on top. This means that if you were to drag race, a two-stroke may get the initial jump from a dead stop if the two-bikes are similar in performance. But the four-stroke

will receive a power surge in midrange and should be able make up ground and beat the other machine to the next obstacle. Of course, this is in general terms, but four-stroke boost is most appreciated toward the end of a straightaway rather than the beginning. This is why four-strokes have traditionally proven to be the most effective motor design when riding in mud and over off-camber terrain, where too much wheelspin can be detrimental.

If the clutch is used too much on a four-stroke, it generally can't withstand the abuse. In most cases, it will overheat and fade quickly. Once this happens, it probably won't

come back during a race and will increase your chances of stalling the engine.

On tight tracks, it's more effective to seek out wider lines that allow you to carry your momentum. This way, you can stay in the meat of the power charge more effectively to the next obstacle. Of course, this depends on the size of the engine and the amount of performance modifications. Rule of thumb is, the larger the motor, the more line choices offered. For example, even though Doug Henry and Jimmy Button ride Yamaha YZ400s, they have to take wider lines in supercross than their 250 two-stroke counterparts. They need a better run at whoops, have to be more

Starts are definitely the strong suit of most four-strokes. These bikes produce less wheelspin and drive harder with less effort from a dead stop than most two-strokes. Here, Craig Anderson (No. 109) grabs the early lead aboard his Yamaha YZ250F.

precise on technical obstacles, and generally find it less beneficial to square off corners.

In contrast, on high-speed outdoor courses, bikes such as the YZ450F and Honda's CRF450R can be ridden in the area of the powerband where power is used more effectively. This means they can seek out more inside lines and aren't as restricted.

One of the major advantages of four-strokes is their ability to corner fast without berms or ruts. Because they accelerate smoothly and don't produce a lot of wheel-spin, they can be ridden effectively on flat turns. Simply roll on the throttle, shift your body weight forward, and hang on for an amazing ride. On high-speed courses, this provides four-stroke riders with more options to shave lap times and make passes.

The biggest disadvantage occurs when four-strokes are required to almost come to a dead stop. It's difficult for riders to not become overaggressive and slip the clutch. Some slippage can be effective, but it must be done briefly and in moderation. Off-road riders who ride in wooded areas will also experience this problem but have a number of ways to deal with the situation. When possible, try to

While fanning the clutch is a key technique on a two-stroke (particularly small-bore bikes), it's not important on a four-stroke. A four-stroke's smooth power delivery allows you to get on the gas earlier in the corner and roll into the powerband rather than clutch into it, as with a two-stroke. Occasionally, of course, even four-stroke riders use the clutch to get to the meat of the powerband. Too much use can cost you the race, however. Once a four-stroke clutch is roasted, you won't get it back until the engine has had plenty of time to cool off.

Because of their increased weight, usually 10–20 pounds more than a two-stroke, thumpers are harder to throw around. Obviously this can be a disadvantage, but new technology is making four-strokes much lighter and more flickable.

Riders such as Doug Henry usually prefer wider corners, especially on supercross-style courses.

avoid coming to a dead stop. Try to maintain enough momentum so you don't run the risk of stalling and can keep instant power on tap.

This is where motor performance really comes into play. High-compression engines, usually associated with a lot of high-performance modifications, can be a double-edged sword. In some cases, they can be great for fast acceleration and minimizing clutch abuse. But on the other hand, they can increase the opportunity for stalling and mandate more clutch use, depending on the situation.

Because high-compression engines offer more engine braking, watch out when jumping. Four-strokes have a tendency to jump front-wheel low if the throttle is chopped too early. This takes a little while to get used to, and it's certainly something to keep in mind.

Braking

Unlike two-strokes, the use of front and rear brakes isn't so important on a thumper. Most four-strokes have enough compression during deceleration to slow the bike down quite

effectively, kind of like a jake brake on a semi truck. This type of braking can be highly effective, but it all depends on engine displacement and motor modifications. Typically, the larger the motor and the higher the compression, the

FOUR-STROKES

Scott Summers—"Avoid half-kicks that many riders use to start two-strokes. Larger four-strokes will only start if you kick them all the way through.

Doug Dubach—"Use the compression release to get the piston just past top dead center to start. The compression release is there for a reason."

Larry Roeseler—"Most four-strokes don't require any throttle to get them started. Be careful not to 'crack' the throttle, like you would on two-strokes. If you're worried that you will do it out of habit, then take your hand off the throttle and place it somewhere else on the handlebar, like on top of your master cylinder."

Randy Hawkins—"If you have a hot-start button, always use it to start a warm bike. It will make carburetion corrections automatically and will save you a lot of hassle."

Dick Burleson—"If you are racing, do everything possible to prevent stalling a bike. A really hot motor can be more difficult to start than a cold one. If you crash, try to keep the clutch in, to keep the engine alive. Having to restart a bike mid-race will zap energy and waste valuable time."

Four-strokes, such as this one ridden by Doug Henry, excel in whoops but usually require a longer approach to build speed effectively for skimming techniques.

faster the engine will slow down a bike.

To use this technique, allow the bike to stay in gear while decelerating, and make sure the clutch is not disengaged. Using this technique gives you more control over the motorcycle, because the dynamic forces of engaging and disengaging the clutch can upset suspension and negatively influence traction. When this happens, riders often back off the throttle too much to make corrections on body positioning. When you use engine braking, you don't have to readjust body positioning as much.

This technique is most effective on flat surfaces, because you're more likely to stall the engine in areas such as whoops or ruts. In most cases, engine braking will cause the rear wheel to slide out slightly while the tire searches desperately for traction. Dirt-track racing riders use engine braking to let the rear wheel step out, in a technique they call "backing it into a corner." On extremely smooth surfaces, this is where four-strokes are much more effective than two-strokes.

Cornering

Because of the type of power delivery and its dislike for clutch abuse, most four-strokes tend to search for wider lines. Though in some instances an inside line can be more effective, the rule of thumb is to go wide. This actually gives you a lot more freedom over two-strokes, or at least gives you different options. However, Honda and Yamaha are trying to make their four-strokes produce two-stroke-like power characteristics, and as this

happens, the bikes will start to handle more like their predecessors.

The biggest advantage of four-strokes is riding on flat ground or off-cambers, because of the smooth power delivery from the four-stroke engine and the lack of wheelspin produced. This is especially true in slippery conditions such as mud or hardpack surfaces.

Four-strokes really don't like to square corners, and this technique is rarely effective. They also don't like being double-clutched or having the clutch slipped for extended periods. But they do like the throttle rolled on with the rider's weight centered over the gas tank and handlebar. They're also effective in shallow ruts, but they usually don't like deep ruts, because the clutch can overheat if the rider isn't careful.

Jumping

Because of engine braking, jumping a thumper can be extremely different from jumping a two-stroke. For starters, many two-stroke riders "chop" the throttle on the face of a jump, instead of powering all the way off the takeoff ramp. If you did this on a four-stroke, you'd most likely find that the bike would slow dramatically and the front end would drop immediately after liftoff. This also has the

Because engine braking makes jumping more difficult, the tendency for four-strokes is to jump front-wheel low. Here, Doug Henry uses engine braking to set up for a rare inside line after this short but steep tabletop.

FOUR-STROKES

- Let the motor help you slow down. Four-strokes offer excellent engine braking.
- Don't abuse the clutch. Four-strokes overheat easily, and most clutches fade when used like a two-stroke.
- Pay attention when chopping the throttle on jump faces. Engine braking may lower the engine too fast and can cause the front end to drop suddenly on takeoff.
- Four-strokes crave flat turns, so don't always seek out ruts and berms as your first two options.
- Power delivery of four-stroke engines provides lots of traction and can be an advantage in mud, off-camber corners, and at motocross-style starts. Remembering this will give you more confidence when racing or riding against two-strokes.

Four-strokes' quick acceleration sometimes makes it tricky to determine correct body position on takeoff for short-approach, high-speed jumps. It can even fool talented riders such as former multi-time National Champion Doug Henry.

tendency to cause riders to jump way short, which can be especially dangerous on short "kicker" jumps.

Still, many riders like to chop the throttle, and this can be okay and safe as long as you make body positioning adjustments to accommodate rapid slowing. Typically, this means shifting your weight to the back of the bike, to keep the front wheel from dropping as the bike becomes airborne.

Suspension

Four-stroke suspension is usually plusher than that of two-strokes. It responds better to small and midsize bumps but doesn't offer the same resistance to bottoming. This is good news for techniques such as engine braking, because it keeps the wheels in contact with the ground more effectively, and it can also

be good for whoops. Generally, four-strokes are more effective in whoops because of smooth power delivery and better rear suspension action.

Unfortunately, because four-strokes are heavier than two-strokes, they also bottom out much more easily. This means that the suspension collapses more on takeoffs, G-outs, big jumps, and poorly timed landings.

In the world of off-road, bikes such as this KTM450 E/XC make an amazing amount of torque that's useful in the woods. In the capable hands of someone such as Dick Burleson, the big-bore thumper can easily loft the front end with a limited amount of wheelspin. This makes it way more predictable to ride than two-strokes. *Ken Faught*

Newspapers, Magazines, Instructional Videos, and Riding Schools

The intention of *Pro Motocross and Off-Road Riding Techniques* is to make you a more informed rider and discuss some of the theories involved in off-road riding. To further enhance your riding skills, you may want to check out some of the motorcycle riding schools, instructional videos, and off-road magazines on the market.

Motorcycle Magazines

Magazines are a great source for tuning tips as well as new-bike tests and product reviews. More important, they're a good way to keep in touch with your sport. All those listed below are monthly. Some can be found at your dealer or at the newsstand; if not, contact the publisher to subscribe.

American Motorcyclist

P.O. Box 6114
Westerville, OH 43081
614-891-2425
www.amadirectlink.com

The publication of the American Motorcyclist Association (AMA), mailed out to members. Street and dirt coverage; great listing of dates, times, and contacts for amateur races and events.

Cycle World

853 W. 17th Street
Costa Mesa, CA 92627
714-720-5300
www.cycleworld.com

General-interest magazine for motorcycle enthusiasts (street-oriented). Includes occasional off-road or motocross bike shootout or test. Occasional off-road product review.

Dirt Bike

25233 Anza Drive
Valencia, CA 91355
805-295-1910
www.dirtbike.com

Covers motocross and off-road riding. New-bike tests, product tests, riding tips, maintenance tips, and race reports.

Dirt Rider

6420 Wilshire Blvd.
Los Angeles, CA 90048-5515
800-800-3478
www.dirtrider.com

Covers motocross and off-road riding. New-bike tests, product tests, riding tips, maintenance tips, race reports. Lists two riding areas each month.

Motocross Action

25233 Anza Drive
Valencia, CA 91355
805-295-1910
www.motocrossactionmag.com

Covers motocross riding. New-bike tests, product tests, maintenance tips, race reports.

Motorcyclist

6420 Wilshire Boulevard
Los Angeles, CA 90048-5515
303-678-0354

General-interest magazine for motorcycle enthusiasts (street bikes only).

Racer X

Route 7, Box 459
Morgantown, WV 26505
304-594-1157
www.racerxill.com

Racy, alternative look at motocross lifestyle.

Sport Rider

6420 Wilshire Boulevard
Los Angeles, CA 90048-5515
303-678-0354

Street bikes only. Hard-core sport riding and racing.

Transworld Motocross

1421 Edinger Avenue, Suite D
Tustin, CA 92780
714-247-0077
www.transworldmotocross.com

Dedicated motocross magazine with mix of lifestyle and tech.

Trail Rider Magazine

P.O. Box 129
Medford, NJ 08055
609-953-7805
www.trailrider.com

Eastern off-road riding and racing. Dual sports. Bike tests.

Moto Playground Magazine

21133 W. 126th Terrace Suite 31
Olathe, KS 66061
785-242-7750
www.motoplayground.com

Motocross-oriented racing magazine.

Internet Sites

The Internet has been steadily improving as a source for dirt bike stuff, including race reports, classifieds, manufacturers, suppliers, and shops. Once you find a few sites, you can check the related links section and find hundreds more. Listed below are some of the biggest and best at the time this book was published. By the time you see this, there will be many more.

Cycle News Site

www.cyclenews.com

Motorcycle news. Race reports (condensed), short features, more.

Dirt Rider site

www.dirtrider.com

Motorcycle news. Race reports (condensed), product tests, legislative issues.

AMA Motocross Championship

www.usmotocross.com

The AMA's official Web site has results, profiles, schedules, more.

Supercross.com

www.supercross.com

Results, schedules, newsletters, Rick Johnson columns, and more about the AMA Supercross series.

Clearchannel Supercross

www.pacesupercross.com

Results, schedules, and live webcasts of world and domestic supercross races.

Motorcycle Books

A number of books are available on motocross and off-road racing. The list below includes some of the better examples. Look for them at your local bookstore, motorcycle dealership, parts store, or on the Internet.

Motocross and Off-Road Motorcycle Performance Handbook, 3rd edition
By Eric Gorr
Motorbooks International, 2004

Turn your motocross or off-road bike into a racing weapon. You'll find everything you need to know and more, from building the ultimate high-rpm outdoor screamer to the inside tips the manual doesn't tell you. Includes specific tuning tips for most off-road bikes as well as suspension tuning, engine tuning, and rebuilding of every system on the bike.

Monkey Butt!
By Rick Sieman
Rick Sieman Racing, 1995

A collection of essays from former *Dirt Bike* magazine editor Rick "Super Hunky" Sieman. Sieman's writing is highly entertaining, and his more serious bits offer an eye-opening look at the motorcycle industry.

Gary Bailey Teaches Rider Technique
By Gary Bailey
Gary Bailey, 1986

Gary Bailey has long been known as the professor of off-road racing technique. In this book he describes his techniques and tactics, with his son, ex-champion David Bailey, demonstrating. This book is a bit long in the tooth, but most of the riding techniques still apply.

A Twist of the Wrist
By Keith Code
Acrobat Books

This classic on road racing techniques has a lot of strategy and mental preparation tips that can be adapted to off-road racing. Don't expect to learn how to clear a triple, but the concepts of ten dollars' worth of attention, focusing on parts of the track you need work on, and developing a strategy to keep racing from driving you to bankruptcy are all applicable.

Major Race Promoters and Sanctioning Bodies

American Motorcyclist Association
P.O. Box 6114
Westerville, OH 43081
614-891-2425
www.ama-cycle.com

National Motosport Association
P.O. Box 46
Norwalk, CA 90650
310-868-8112
www.nmamx.com

Racer Productions
Route 7, Box 459
Morgantown, WV 26505
304-594-1157
www.racerproductions.com

Riding Schools and Instruction Video Distributors

Gary Bailey Video/MX Schools
P.O. Box 130
Axton, VA 24054
703-650-1759
www.garybailey.com

Tony D Motocross Schools
345 John Hyde Rd.
New Windsor, MD 21776
410-635-6916
www.tonydmxschool.com

Donnie Hansen Motocross Academy
1174 Whitney Dr.
Yuba City, CA 95991
916-755-2799
www.dhma.com

Mike Healey MX School
3209 Colorado Pl.
Costa Mesa, CA 92626
714-435-1741

Rick Johnson MX School of Champions
P.O. Box 80
Trabuco Canyon, CA 92678
949-951-7223
www.mxschoolofchampions.com

Gary Semics Motocross School
37316 Eagleton Road
Lisbon, OH 44432

Phone: 330-424-9295
Fax: 330-424-8052
E-mail: gary@gsmxs.com
www.gsmxs.com

Marty Smith Motocross Clinic
2486 Eltinge Dr.
Alpine, CA 91901
619-659-0273
www.martysmithmotocross.com

If you've been wanting to go to a motocross school but there hasn't been one in your area at the right time, the Gary Semics Motocross School has a solution. Gary is training and certifying instructors to teach under his school's name and format. As of March 2004, there are six active instructors:

Dean Olsen
Montana (will travel)
406-458-8164
dolsen@gsmxs.com

Jeff Sanford
California, Northwest Ohio, Michigan
419-392-6425
jsanford282@aol.com

David Kilgore
Ohio (will travel)
330-424-9295
david@gsmxs.com

Kris Papworth
Utah and Western United States
714-883-8120
gsmx@hotmail.com

Jorge Martin
Argentina, South America (will travel)
02 944 432930
jmarti@bariloche.com.ar

Alfredo Abreu
Dominican Republic
809-547-1057
alfrabre@tricom.net

Instructional Videos & DVDs

Gary Semics Videos
(800-500-3938, 330-424-9295,
www.gsmxs.com)

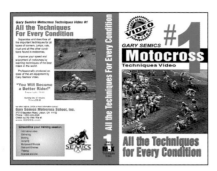

Gary Semics Techniques Video and DVD #1
All the Techniques for Every Condition
Tape No. V1, 1992

You'll learn the techniques for sweeping, bermed, banked, and off-camber corners, handling rough downhills, general jumping techniques, plus jumping in ruts, riding in the mud, and many other conditions found in motocross. 37 minutes

Gary Semics Techniques Video and DVD #2
The Rider and Motorcycle . . . Making the Two Become One
Tape No. V2, 1993

Video 2 combines all the techniques into the two most important fundamentals—maintaining the center of balance and mastering the use of all five controls—and shows ways to practice them. These fundamentals are described in a stationary position, in a set-up practice situation, and in race action by the superstars. Both the correct way and the most common mistakes are shown. You'll learn about what every motocrosser is striving for: riding in "total flow concentration." 60 minutes

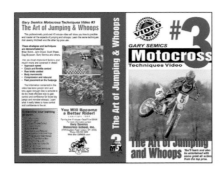

Gary Semics Techniques Video and DVD #3
The Art of Jumping and Whoops!
Tape No. V3, 1994

Learn and be entertained at the same time with major air and cross-ups from some of the best racers in the business. Learn how to master all aspects of jumping and whoops using the same techniques Jeremy McGrath and other top pros use! 40 minutes

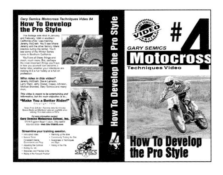

Gary Semics Techniques Video and DVD #4
How to Develop the Pro Style
Tape No. V4, 1996

This video was shot during winter pre-season training in southern California while Gary was training Jeremy McGrath. You'll see where Jeremy and the other factory riders practice during the winter, some of the Winter Series races in Southern California, and how the number one 125 intermediate racer in the country—16-year-old Jerry Dostal, trained by Gary Semics since he was 11—approaches racing.

You'll learn all about the important body positions and movements and how they apply to all aspects of motocross, how to use the front brake, some great practice drills for improving body movements quickly and effectively, and some of the important dos and don'ts of motocross. 60 minutes

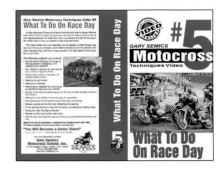

Gary Semics Techniques Video and DVD #5
What to Do on Race Day
Tape No. V5, 1997

In this video, you'll see a lot of action, from the local level to the Pro National Level, and the steps to follow from the day before through race day. The trick is to race the kind of race you're capable of racing, to race at your highest potential. Be ready when the gate drops, because that's when the nonsense stops. 40 minutes

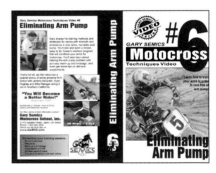

Gary Semics Techniques Video and DVD #6
Eliminating Arm Pump
Tape No. V6, 1997

Here's a simple forearm workout program that will condition your arms for motocross. Gary shares his time-tested methods and strategies for racing with strength and endurance in your arms, not lactic acid arm pump. You'll also see some extreme action with Jeremy McGrath, Ryan Hughes, and Mike Metzger airing it out in Southern California. 21 minutes

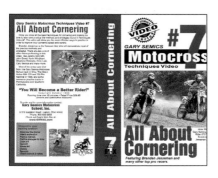

Gary Semics Techniques Video and DVD #7
All About Cornering
Tape No. V7, 1998

This video will show you the most effective ways to practice so as to improve your cornering speed and control. Branden Jesseman is the featured rider and demonstrates most of the practice methods and strategies. You'll also see Jeremy McGrath, John Dowd, Kevin Windham, Ezra Lusk, Gary Semics, and many more. Most of the action was shot at the GSMXS Motocross School Track in Ohio, the Glenn Helen AMA 125 and 250 Pro National in 1998, and at some awesome practice tracks in Pennsylvania and Southern California. 45 minutes

Gary Semics Techniques Video and DVD #8
Bike Setup
Tape No. V8, 2000

This video covers all the important adjustments every bike needs. You'll gain speed and confidence when all the components of your motorcycle are set up properly. Here's what you'll learn:

Carburetor: how to test and set the jetting

Suspension: springs for your weight, spring pre-load, and clicker adjustments for front and rear suspension (rebound and compression)

Chassis: setting the height of the fork tubes in the triple clamps

Tires: selection and pressure

Demo riders in this video are Branden Jesseman, David Kilgore, and Gary Semics, along with many others from Amateur National and Pro National competition. 47 minutes

MX Conditioning Video and DVD
Training and Diet with Gary Semics
Training and diet manual included
2003

This motocross conditioning video and manual combo package includes all Gary Semics' latest training and diet information to make you a lean, mean racing machine, including the best training and diet programs he used to train Jeremy McGrath and many of the other top pros. 90 minutes

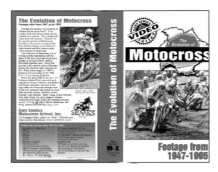

The Evolution of Motocross
Tape No. VE 1996

Forty-eight years of motocross are covered in this fascinating history of the sport. See the legends of motocross in their prime as they form what is today's motocross racing. Video footage begins with European racing in 1947 and covers the history of MX all the way to scenes of Jeremy McGrath on his private practice track. 95 minutes

These tapes from Racing Solutions offer insight from a few of the sport's greatest racers.

Steve Lamson's Racing Techniques: The Champ Reveals His Speed Secrets
Racing Solutions
949-582-0351, ext. 2

Two-time 125cc AMA National Champion Steve Lamson explains motocross techniques in depth—everything from starts to cornering, jumping, and more. This is a great video for riders of all skill levels. 40 minutes

Greg Albertyn's Factory Bike Setup Secrets
Racing Solutions video or DVD
949-582-0351, ext. 2

Explains the bike setup information Greg Albertyn used to win three World Championships and the 1999 AMA 250cc National Motocross Championship. Helpful for riders and mechanics of all skill levels, documented in an easy-to-understand manner. 40 minutes

Freestyle Insanity: Trevor Vines Explains How He Pulls These Wicked Tricks
Racing Solutions
949-582-0351, ext. 2

Trevor Vines, the first full-time factory-backed freestyle motocross rider, explains exactly what it takes for him to pull off these insane moves step-by-step in a way that makes it easy to understand.

Glossary

Aftermarket parts: Parts produced by a company other than the original equipment manufacturer.

Bore: One dimension of an engine's cylinder.

cc: Abbreviation for cubic centimeter.

Cross-rutted: What happens when one wheel accidentally comes out of a rut.

Double: Two jumps in succession taken in one leap.

Endo: Abbreviation of "end over end": a bike uncontrollably flipping over frontward.

Ergonomics: The relationship between man and machine.

Four-stroke: A piston engine that fires every fourth stroke. Intake and exhaust are controlled with mechanically actuated valves. Power output from these engines is typically smoother and more controllable than two-stroke engines, but the valvetrain makes the engines heavier.

Gyroscopic: A gyroscope is an object spinning on an axis. The gyroscopic effect is essential in many cases for maintaining balance on a motorcycle.

Hardpack: Extremely hard terrain that provides little traction.

Headshake: When the handlebars shake uncontrollably from side to side.

High-side: The action that occurs when a rider falls over on the outside while leaning into a turn or swapping out of control.

Hot line: Slang for the best line choice.

Knobbies: The small portion of tire tread that creates traction. Knobbies come in a wide range of patterns for all types of off-road riding.

Loop-out: When the front wheel comes so high off the ground that the bike flips over backward.

Low-side: The action that occurs when a rider falls over on the inside while leaning into a turn.

Master link: The connecting point of the drive chain.

MX: Abbreviation for motocross.

Nosedive: The attitude of a bike when the front wheel is substantially lower than the rear wheel.

Open bike: Typically a machine with a displacement of 251cc or larger.

Outcropping: A clump of earth, usually rock, that sticks off the side of a mountain.

Overrev: The act of allowing an engine to exceed its effective rpm range.

Powerband: The useful power of an engine. The powerband stretches from bottom end (low rpm) through midrange to top end (high rpm).

Preload: The force applied to a spring at rest. Generally used in reference to fork and shock springs.

Pre-run: Riding the course before the race to get an idea of the terrain, layout, speeds, and so on.

R&D: Abbreviation for "research and development."

Sag: How much suspension drops when a bike is not being ridden and is off the stand. Sag is usually measured in millimeters and plays an important role in motorcycle setup.

Shim: A thin piece of metal used to take up space.

Sidewalls: The sides of the tire where there are knobs.

Square off: Turning extremely sharply with the rear wheel locked up.

Swap: The uncontrollable action when the rear wheel of a motorcycle bounces from side to side.

Swingarm: The large metallic object that connects the rear wheel to the frame and the shock.

Tabletop: A jump similar to a double, with both takeoff and landing ramps but having the middle section filled with dirt.

Tacky: A description of soil that provides traction so good it's almost sticky.

Trials: A type of motorcycle riding and competition that requires precise balance to negotiate a wide range of jagged, slippery, and odd-shaped obstacles at extremely slow speeds. Participants are penalized for dabbing a foot. Each rider rides the course solo, and points are tallied after riders complete a series of courses. Riders are timed, in case it's necessary to decide a tie.

Triple: Three jumps in succession taken in one leap.

Triple clamp: The portion of the motorcycle that connects the handlebar to the frame and the fork.

Two-stroke: A piston engine that fires on every other stroke. Intake and exhaust are controlled with ports in the cylinder. Modern engines typically use reed valves in the intake tract and mechanically operated exhaust valves that change the size of the exhaust port.

Wheelbase: The distance between the front and back wheels.

Index

**Jeremy McGrath: Images of a
Motocross Champion**
ISBN 0-7603-2032-2

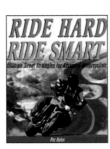

**Ride Hard, Ride Smart:
Ultimate Street Strategies
for Advanced Motorcyclists**
ISBN 0-7603-1760-7

Ten Days in the Dirt
ISBN 0-7603-1803-4

Dirt Rider's
Motocross Riding Tips
ISBN 0-7603-1315-6

**Freestyle Motocross II:
Air Sickness**
ISBN 0-7603-1184-6

**Motocross Racers:
30 Years of Legendary
Dirt Bikes**
ISBN 0-7603-1239-7

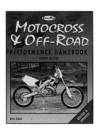

**Motocross and Off-Road
Performance Handbook**
ISBN 0-7603-0660-5

Streetbike Extreme
ISBN 0-7603-1299-0

**Freestyle Motocross:
Jump Tricks from the Pros**
ISBN 0-7603-0926-4